D0273118

Contributors: K Griffiths & J Pitt
Design and Illustrations by Naomi Maister

ISBN 978-0-9561238-0-0

Introduction

Some time back I went for drinks with friends and conversation moved from how depressing the recession is to how to beat it. Interestingly, it turned out that nearly every person around the table was doing something on the side. From eBay wheeler-dealer to doing ladies' nails in the evenings to ticket touting to outsourced component manufacture (that was a strange one), everybody around the table was making a bit extra – even the guy behind the bar was flogging hair straighteners.

Was this phenomenon more widespread or do I just gravitate to entrepreneurial type people? I rang round my friends and dug a little deeper and it became clear that my immediate social circle is not an isolated cluster of Del Boys and Rodneys.

Indeed, nearly everyone I know is making money doing other things not related to their day job or are, at the least, putting significant thought into exploring avenues that may yield the 'odd quid to pay for a holiday'. So I put a notice up on Facebook to see if I could collect these ideas into a guide and publish them. However, so possessive are we of our little money-making schemes that nobody replied. Either that or my so-called 'friends' don't really like me and couldn't be bothered to help. That's the thing about Facebook. If you want to know what colour underpants someone you went to school with 25 years ago is wearing at this moment in time it's great. If you actually want to know anything useful then forget it.

When Napoleon famously commented that "*L'Angleterre est une nation de boutiquiers*" he wasn't far wrong. For thousands of years the Brits have been buying and selling stuff. As an island nation our empire was built on trade and our status as serious world player continues to be underpinned by it. It's wired into the DNA of every one of us that is proud to call him or herself British. Del and Rodney Trotter are national heroes because week after week they got up and tried to make a living any which way they could with an unyielding energy for doing deals that boshed a bit of extra wonga in the jar.

So walk tall, fellow Brit, you're in good company. There is money to be made, a recession to be beaten and a couple of quid to be made on the side. And this tome is going to give you some ideas as to how you can go about it. It probably won't pave the way to fabulous riches (although undoubtedly some of these schemes could be successful and develop into very lucrative ways to make you a living – it would be tempting to ditch your job in customer complaints to make £50K a year flogging hot spuds) but it might pay for a new car, bolster your battered pension, finance a nice holiday, help fund that conservatory you've always wanted or simply pay the latest incomprehensively massive gas bill. ●

TELL US ABOUT IT!

Tell us about your successes or failures or simply share your experiences if you have put any of these ideas into practice. Also if there are other money-making ideas you want to share with our readers then don't keep them to yourself. Visit our website at www.101Guides.co.uk and share your thoughts and ideas about how to make an extra bit of cash.

Recession . n. a temporary economic decline during which trade and industrial activity are reduced.

A Guide to Surviving the Recession

Firstly, let's get some perspective on this recession thing

This is a bad time but it will pass quickly. We all know roughly why it's happened and to a degree we're all partly to blame, although the bankers deserve the lion's share of it obviously. So put down that cudgel and stop hanging around outside Northern Rock and let's not dwell on the past and look to the future.

By 2015 what is making you worry now will be but a distant memory and you will look back through the fog of time and wonder what all the fuss was about.

By 2050 there will most certainly have been another recession, possibly two, even three and you'll be an old hand at dealing with them. You will laugh in the face of monetary meltdown.

By 2100 you will almost certainly be dead. Sorry to be blunt but it's true.

By 2200 you will most likely be completely and totally forgotten other than an entry on a family tree, a profile on Facebook or a dusty photo on a wall.

By 5000AD it is likely that the human race will be extinct. Forget global warming, our explosive rate of population growth is not sustainable and nature will correct it. Nature corrects, that's what it does.

Sixty million years hence a new species will be digging up your fossilised remains, polishing them and putting them in a museum. Experts will speculate how you were probably green in colour, almost certainly evolved from gerbils and more than likely spent your time mindlessly attacking other humans because you only had brains, laughably, the size of a melon.

In just under a billion years time the earth will be engulfed by the sun as it expands in its final spectacular death throes. After that the sun will go out and become a purposeless lump of dull rock drifting in the frozen void.

So, you, everyone else around you, everything that is important to you right now is a temporary state of affairs that really has no significance in the greater universe. A few years of economic uncertainty is not going to affect that so you might as well pick yourself up, stop worrying, be nice to those around you and think of ways to get through it.

It is all about the money so you might as well resign yourself to it

Now, no matter how much we try and think of ways around it, in this world of ours it is all about the money. Unfortunate. But true. It's not just about power and influence and a nice car on the drive. It's the very bedrock on which our society sits. It's the glue that binds us together and enables trade and its bedfellow, peace, to flourish all around the world.

One could argue that much of the world is in conflict but I can assure you that without money the conflict would be infinitely worse and the world would be a far more uncertain and vicious place. In our short history humans have tried many ways of co-existing and interacting harmoniously and the stability that money brings seems to be the best way of achieving this.

In early history if you wanted something you simply took it. Twenty thousand years ago two tribes encountering each other on the open plain were unlikely to greet each other with a "hail fellow, well met". There would have been a brutal skirmish, one tribe would have got the upper hand, slaughtered all the males, taken the women, livestock, ipods, anything else of value and destroyed the rest. This is not a productive model for a superior race of beings to adopt and something had to change otherwise we would spend all our time bashing each other's skulls in instead of pursuing such useful pastimes as inventing the wheel or the Rubik Cube.

Look around you at your fellow animals and unremitting unsentimental brutality is the natural order of things. The strong survive. The weak get eaten. If you think a recession is stressful try going to sleep in a cold cave, bat poo dripping on your head, cowed with the fear that your next-door neighbour is going to club you to death and take your wife and collection of bones.

As our species became more enlightened we discovered the notion of organised trade and bartering became the accepted method of exchange. The downside of this is that if you didn't particularly like turnips and your client was a turnip farmer it created a problem. Sure, you could take the turnips and then swap them for something else, like a couple of pints of mead, but it meant hauling a load of turnips down to the pub which, let's face it, is not really convenient. So eventually around 1000BC the Romans cooked up this idea of money where coins or paper became a store of value and we didn't have to cart around turnips anymore. This did have the unfortunate side effect of creating that breed of people called bankers and their more sinister cousins – financial advisers. As I have said, money is the best of a bad bunch.

So we're stuck with money as a way of managing our lives; it's essential to keep a roof over our head and put food on the table and we need to keep earning it. Even through the bad times. So face up to it. If I've brought your mood down with this matter of fact outlook don't worry because I'm about to pick you up and get you started on your road to making an extra couple of quid.

Because it's not all bad!

A recession is unlikely to kill you (unless you are a stockbroker jumping out of the window of a Wall Street skyscraper. Although there is evidence that only one person ever did this in 1920 and he was said to have had emotional issues before the crash and was labouring under the misapprehension that he was an eagle. It should also be noted that most of us don't work in skyscrapers and even if we did when was the last time you went in a skyscraper that had windows that actually opened?) so we all really need to take a deep breath and put your best foot forward.

Remember this:

You live in a Free Country which operates a Free Market Economy. This is a good thing because YOU can make a difference. YOU can take control of your own destiny. Your income is dictated by how versatile you are and how hard you are prepared to work. You have the power to singlehandedly change your circumstances.

Also most recessions only last a few years so the banks will be chucking money at us again in no time.

Another benefit of this period of fiscal turbulence is that it will curb your habit of buying junk you don't need. Did you really need that Swedish stacking box set? Or has that MP3 speaker docking system for the bathroom really changed your life? Thought not.

We've become so used to buying stuff we don't need that it will do us the world of good to cease doing it. None of it makes our lives better.

Just because the economic climate is miserable does not mean that opportunities do not exist.

Walt Disney opened his studio doors during the recession of 1923, Hewlett Packard began life during the Depression, and Bill Gates and Paul Allen founded Microsoft amid the 1970s oil crisis.

There is always money to be made in good times and bad.

Recessions jumble things up. Big companies will suffer with their large payrolls, big offices with high rents and cost bases that are hard to trim but this is a golden time for people who have good ideas, low overheads and the ability to work hard and move quickly. A recession changes the natural order of things. There are opportunities everywhere.

Prepare for change

This book is about changing your outlook and your working patterns. If you're not prepared to change your 9–5, Monday to Friday mentality then go and change this for a copy of *Heat Magazine*.

Possibly the most immediate change you can make right now is to get rid of your telly. Sell it. It will make you your first bit of extra cash on the side. British people on average spend four hours a day watching television. That's 28 hours a week. If you convert this wasted time into the minimum wage (at the time of writing this is

£5.73 for people over 22) this alone equates to £8342 per annum. If you put this 28 hours per week towards a money-making scheme who knows where it will take you?

If your TV has no value then take it out into the garden and put a hammer through the screen. It might not make you any money but it will feel brilliant and make a statement that you intend to dedicate yourself to making money.

Some tips and advice

Magazine and local newspapers have been hit very hard by the arrival of the internet. It has drained one of their main sources of revenue: advertising. This means their advertising rates have crashed over the past few years. Promoting your services in the local media can be very cost effective, with many papers now offering free or very cheap advertising in their classified sections. Use them. Local newspapers are still widely read and they are a great way to get your offering in front of the right people.

A Word from David Moffat of Moffat & Gilbert Chartered Accountants, top tax accountant and my brother's father-in-law, who has  **spent many years assisting people in divvying up their hard earned booty and sharing it with the tax man, grrrr.**

It is beyond the scope of this brief article to go into detail about our tax system, and what follows is intended to draw the reader's attention to the tax and National Insurance implications which attach to the kind of earnings envisaged by this book. Essentially these are likely to be self-employed earnings.

Everyone who is employed, self-employed or retired will pay income tax on their annual income and, if under 65 years of age for a man and 60 for a woman, National Insurance contributions.

Those people who already complete a tax return because they are in receipt of other income will each year thus include within that return, details of their self-employed income. Those who are becoming self-employed for the first time, which may include people who are drawing state benefits, will need to inform the Inland Revenue of the fact that they are becoming self-employed.

This is best achieved by accessing the Inland Revenue's website www.hmrc.gov.uk/Selfemployed which explains in simple terms the steps which need to be taken. Alternatively, the Inland Revenue Newly Self-employed Helpline may be telephoned on 0845 915 4515 for advice on how to proceed. It should be emphasised that penalties may be incurred if the Inland Revenue is not notified within three months that self-employment has commenced.

Avoid internet scams that offer you untold riches for little work – there are lots of charlatans on the internet and it's not just the obvious ones where the Minister for Foreign Affairs in Nigeria is trying to pay you $12 million for helping him shift the country's gold reserves through your Halifax Instant Savers account. On a basic level handing over your personal details can be annoying as you'll be swamped by spam. On a more serious note many of the get rich quick schemes require you to spend money to register. There is nothing wrong with speculating to accumulate but most of these schemes are a con and should be avoided. I'm afraid, folks, that honest toil is the best policy.

If you already have a job and are trying to supplement it beware that sometimes your employee contract can preclude you from pursuing other lines of work. Check if this is the case and take appropriate action if your contract does prevent you from taking on extracurricular activities. Options:

Don't do it.

Ask your employer if it's OK to do it.

Don't tell your employer (or your mates in the canteen) that you're doing it.

Remember the tax man. We live in a free country with opportunities available to every man but we also have a ruthless and unforgiving tax system. You play it by the book and you'll be fine but try and fiddle Her Maj's tax inspectors and they'll hang, draw and quarter you and then send you a bill for hanging, drawing and quartering.

So put the kettle on, open a nice pack of digestives and browse through the 101 ideas we've come up with which could help you make an extra couple of quid. Not all of them will be suitable to each reader but we are sure you will find something. And remember to let us know how you get on at **www.101guides.co.uk**. Your success will inspire other readers to join you in beating this recession.●

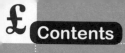

The List

Contents £

1
B&B

This is not available to everyone but if you do have a few spare rooms, live in a location where there is a tourist demand and are handy with a frying pan then why not join the 20,000 other Brits who run a B&B. Average revenue from a room is about £75 per night and dedicated B&B'ers can generate up to £40K a year through two rooms.

It's hard work though and you definitely have to be a people person. People who enjoy meeting strangers and can immerse themselves in the business will find it a rewarding way to increase their income, those who are only doing it for the money should watch *Fawlty Towers* before taking this any further.

With any business involving the general public being on your premises there is a raft of legislative box ticking including insurance cover, planning regulations, fire certificates, health and safety and food hygiene. You may incur building costs to bring you up to scratch with fire regulations and there will also be investment required in marketing. You can register with your local tourist office and it would be an advantage to have your own website which should cost you about £300–£500 pounds to have set up . If you have a steady flow of cars or people coming past your house you could opt for the tried and tested method of sticking up a B&B sign.

Useful info: there are many websites dedicated to walking you through those first tentative steps into the hospitality industry: www.startabedandbreakfast.co.uk and www. howtorunabandb.com

Tips: go and stay in a B&B for a night and ask the owners what the life is like

Risk	💣💣
Return	£££
Time	⏰⏰⏰⏰⏰
Training	📖📖

2
Babysitting

The average fee in this country for babysitting is £5 an hour and it's not just fit for 14-year-old girls. Not bad when you consider that this usually entails eating crisps, watching Sky and using someone else's central heating. Except don't take the responsibility lightly.

Like the fire service most of the time you're hanging around but when that fire starts you need to be prepared to deal with it. When a baby starts to cry you need to know that you can handle the situation and act quickly. From simply tucking an infant back in with its teddy to comforting a hysterical child to dealing with accidents around the home you should have experience in dealing with children. If you don't like children or responsibility then give this one a miss and try beating (below).

You also need to be cautious as to how you promote yourself and get customers. Putting cards in a local newsagent's window is not always the best way as there can be some odd people out there. In the first instance you should consider your safety. We suggest printing off a few letters and posting them through letterboxes of those houses in your immediate local vicinity, to people that are known to you and your neighbours.

Once you've got a job tell people you are babysitting and leave details of where you are going to be and the anticipated time you will return. Once you've got a regular job then ask the parents (your customers) if they can spread the word. Word of mouth referrals get you the best rates and a higher degree of personal security by staying in a social network.

Another plus with babysitting is that it takes you out of your comfortable home environment so is often a good place to combine it with another money-making activity.

Tips: think safety

Risk	💣💣💣💥
Return	££
Time	🕐🕑
Training	📖

3
Baked potato selling

Ahh, the simplicity of a baked spud on a cold winter's day. Sweaters as goal posts and [insert your favourite childhood nostalgic item in here]. We all love a jacket spud.

The tuber of the potato plant was first cultivated high up in the Andes about 7000 years ago. The first potato crossed the Atlantic some time in 1570 and the first chip shop opened in Madrid in 1571 when someone invented those funny little wooden fork things that don't pick up chips very well. The convenience of a food that comes wrapped in its own cooking jacket bursting with vitamins and carbohydrates must have been a marvel when it arrived in Europe and so popular did it become that by 1750 Ireland had become totally dependent on it for feeding itself. When the entire crop failed in the mid-1800s it caused widespread famine and a mass exodus of Irish to the USA. And Kilburn.

An acquaintance recently explained to me the financials of running a potato stand (which he started to do at the weekend and now does it full time because it makes a shed load more than being in poxy IT). To give a person a piping hot spud, with a knob of butter, a sprinkling of cheese, one of those funny polystyrene cases that you always see crushed up alongside the motorway, a flimsy plastic knife and fork and a water repellent non-absorbent napkin costs about 50p. He sells them for £1.95. And he charges an extra 50p for the topping.

The basic sums:

You sell 100

£1.95 - £0.50 = £1.45 margin x 100 sales = £ 145

That's it folks. You can make £145 per day in cash. And that's before you sell the topping and fizzy pop to go with it.

You will need to buy a commercial spud oven which costs between £200 for a second hand one and £7000 for the king of spud bakers. In some instances you may need to pay for a space (say at a market or carboot sale) or need a license (if you wanted to do it on the high street). Some ovens also have a hot water supply which means you can sell tea. The seven grand machines come built into

their own trailer and will knock out hundreds of potatoes per day but this is obviously a big risk and we suggest starting small.

Raw materials can be purchased from a local food wholesaler (spuds, beans, other toppings, cheese, environmentally unfriendly plastic stuff) and the ovens can be purchased new from catering companies or check out eBay for some used bargains. This can be undertaken as a part-time weekend activity servicing carboots, fun fairs, weekend markets, farmers' markets or concerts or you can even start a full-time career with a regular pitch in a town centre. Some people have even been known to buy a few machines and hire students to do the standing around in the cold bit.

Tips: remember you'll need to keep things clean if you're selling food to the general public. Find the local markets and plan your year ahead before buying an oven – it's no good spending hundreds of pounds on gear only to find your local spud market is sewn up. Prepare to get cold

Risk	
Return	££
Time	⏱ ⏱ ⏱
Training	📖

4
Beating

The trouble with pheasants is they don't particularly like being shot at. Indeed they are particularly loathe to take flight when 15 tweed-clad bankers are waiting 20 feet away with loaded 12 gauges ready to blow them out of the sky. Similarly tweed-clad bankers don't like schlepping all the way up to Norfolk for a day's killing and finding that there is nothing to kill. They get cross because they could have spent their time more effectively in London withdrawing overdraft facilities from small companies or dreaming up ways of selling dodgy loans to my granddad's pension fund. Enter the beater.

The beater gets paid to walk in front of the shooters bashing bushes and hedgerows with sticks and generally scaring the pheasants so they flee in fear, instinctively launching themselves upwards and straight into the cross-hairs of the waiting shooters.

The shoot organizers are happy because they are providing the service they promised, namely big flappy lumbering slow birds a few feet away from the end of a gun, the shooters are happy because they get to maim wildlife and the beaters are happy because they get fed and watered during the shoot, are paid anything between £15 and £50 per day depending on location and usually get to take home a brace or two of the kill saving you money on your supper. As an added bonus most butchers will pay a couple of quid for the pheasants if you're not into eating game.

Watching wildlife be torn apart by tiny lead pellets directly above your head is not everyone's idea of a day well spent. But if you like that sort of thing this can be a fun day out and make you a couple of quid. The grouse season starts 12 August and finishes 10 December, pheasants start 1 October and finish 1 February. If you like the whole gun thing, off-season you could do some work at clay pigeon shoots – pressing buttons when folk shout "Pull!" Simple.

Useful info: for information on your local shoots and other jobs in the beating and picking-up business contact, www.nobs.org.uk (seriously)

Tips: wear ear plugs

Risk

Return £

Time

Training

5
Beer making

When I was a boy my friend Tarquin used to make his own beer and one batch made us go mad and caused temporary sight loss. One of our gang thought he was an orange and tried to peel himself and then it all got a bit like *The Day of the Triffids*. So making beer is something that should not be done by impatient 16-year-old boys with too much time on their hands.

However, our research has uncovered a very interesting way of turning a love of beer into a hobby or even a business that can be profitable and be fantastically interesting. Before reading further you must understand that you need to invest a not insubstantial amount of cash into this scheme. It's not like babysitting. And you're going to be buying a brewery.

In my house I know that there is nothing that would annoy the wife more than me coming home at the end of the day, as she's had her brain frazzled by looking after two young children, to be told that I've bought a vintage Porsche. That would make her cross. The only thing that would make her even more cross would be to tell her that I've used our life savings to buy, er, a micro brewery. Yes, darling, but, you see, it can pay itself back in a year. Possibly two. And you've always said I needed a hobby...

So, on the minus side your wife will hate you and probably kick you out. But you will find male friends flocking to your newly acquired bedsit to hear about your new enterprise.

THE BLOKE

ATTENTION BLOKES!

DO YOU ANSWER YES TO THE FOLLOWING THREE QUESTIONS?!?!?!

- IS THE CREDIT CRUNCH GETTING YOU DOWN?
- DO YOU REMEMBER A TIME WHEN YOU USED TO LAUGH?
- WOULD YOU LIKE TO GET A BRILLIANT, WITTY, AMUSING, IRREVERANT, SARCASTIC AND THOUGHT PROVOKING MAGAZINE DIRECT TO YOUR INBOX EVERY THURSDAY - FOR FREE?

THIS IS WHAT YOU GET

- FUNNY VIDS
- GADGET REVIEWS
- BETTING TIPS
- A WRY LOOK AT LIFE
- MICKEY TAKING

LIKE THOSE EMAILS YOU GET FROM YOUR MATES - EXCEPT WITH MORE STUFF!

THIS IS WHAT YOU WON'T GET

- ENTICING OFFERS TO HELP MOVE £10 BILLION FROM THE NIGERIAN MINISTER OF THE INTERIOR'S BANK ACCOUNT
- PROMISES TO MAKE YOUR WILLY BIGGER
- NO IN-DEPTH DISSECTION OF HOW THE CREDIT CRUNCH WILL TOTALLY SCREW UP YOUR LIFE

TO SIGN UP, VISIT WWW.THEBLOKE.CO.UK

is a need for your product. If there is already a microbrewer servicing the pubs in your area then think again (or is there room for two). Similarly if there are no pubs or freehold pubs in your area then this probably won't work either

Risk	🧨🧨🧨🧨🧨
Return	££
Time	🕐🕐🕐
Training	📖📖

6
Blogging

So what is a microbrewery? It is a small scale commercial brewing plant. There are about 400 in the UK and several hundred in the US. The leading supplier of plants is a firm in Yorkshire called Mossbrew which is run by Graham Moss (pictured above). There are various types of plant available from the humble 90L Pilot (£2499) right up to the 1600L 10 Barrel (£39,950) but you could get yourself in business with a 2.5L Barrel which costs £8750. Delivery takes up to eight weeks and it is recommended that you take a three day introductory brewing course for £399 which will be enough to teach you about the techniques to produce different beers and not blind people and the mountain of legislation that comes with making food and drink for the public.

Many freehold pubs buy directly from microbreweries and if you can manage to produce a good brew then it is likely that you can develop a lucrative local market. A successful brewer will also find a ready market to introduce new products.

Useful info: the marvellous Mosssbrew.co.uk

Tips: do some local research to establish if there

If you have no interest in the internet and don't own a computer this one is probably not for you. Blogs, or web logs, are increasingly becoming a viable way to make money. You're not going to make enough to retire, but then this is not what this is about. A blog is essentially an online diary where you tell the world what you are doing and you invite the world to comment on what you are doing. Some blogs are read by millions of people each day, others are only read by a handful. I have a blog called TheBloke.co.uk which is read by about 50 people a day.

Advertisers on the internet are interested in only one thing: the right kind of traffic.

Think of it like having a shop. As an example, let us say your shop sells hamsters. There is no point in filling your shop with thousands of people that have no intention of purchasing a hamster. They clutter the place up muttering about all the hamsters and make you feel bad about your business. You want to attract a particular kind of person with a keen interest in small rodents because he is more likely to spend money – to become a CUSTOMER.

So from an internet perspective you want to display your advert to hamster lovers. Let's say for argument sake, and taking this example to its conclusion, that you find a small blog called www.weLoveHamsters.com. Not many people visit the site but every single one is interested in small furry critters.

This is the perfect audience and you would be happy to pay good money to advertise to this small but very relevant group. This is the very essence of the internet and why it's become so successful, it's very good at pointing advertising at the right type of people.

So set up a blog discussing something you like, say fishing. Most blogging software is free and easy to operate. Invite your fishing chums to visit and trade comments and insults about fishing and all things fishing related. If you update your blog regularly and you write interesting things more people will come and have a look and before long you will have built up a little community of like-minded people. Once you have achieved this you can then sign up online with a company that will pay you money to put their advert on your site. Income can range from a few $ to many thousands of $ a month (because the internet is global many companies price in US dollars).

Although it is hard to get precise figures, one US blog called 'Ask the Builder' is estimated to generate up to $1 million per annum and one of the best known gossip bloggers, Perez Hilton, is supposed to earn an annual income anywhere between $500,000 and $800,000. Very lucrative indeed.

Useful info: for setting up a free blog check out www.wordpress.com or www.mykindablog.co.uk. For selling ads on your blog www.bloggingads.com or www.money-from-blogs.com

Tips: choose a topic for your blog rather than a general rant about how rubbish your life is.

Try and write about something that interests you such as your hobby, leisure activity or job as it makes it easier to update if you enjoy what you are blogging about

Risk	💣
Return	£
Time	☺ ☺ ☺ ☺
Training	📖

7
Book keeping

The UK has four million small businesses employing about half of the UK workforce. Every single one of these must 'do books' – which translates to submitting a set of accounts to the government at the end of the financial year, tax returns, payroll services – and every single one of these people likes to have someone around them who has a modicum of financial competence. Are you that person?

If you are organized, have a head for figures, attention to detail, a responsible attitude and have some basic computer skills then this could be for you. You can't just wake up one morning and call yourself a book keeper and this option will require investment in time and money. The rewards however can be significant and it can provide the kind of flexibility that suits many people. You can fit it in around the kids or develop it into a full-time career.

A newly qualified book keeper can earn between £10–£15 per hour. A basic starter home course can be taken in as little as two weeks and costs about £300. More advanced courses can then be taken as you become more experienced and of course the more experienced you are the more you can charge.

A local chamber of commerce will be able to assist with marketing and you should also go to local business networking events (remember to get some business cards). Once you have a client ask them to ask their friends. Word of mouth is king in this industry.

Useful info: check out the Institute of Chartered Book Keepers at www.book-keepers.org

Tips: talk to your local commercial estate agent to see if he will tip you off when companies take a new office lease. It's the best time to get a new client – when they are starting out

Risk	
Return	££
Time	ⓟ ⓟ ⓟ ⓟ
Training	📖 📖 📖

8
Breastfeeding consultant

Sorry chaps, this one is not for you. Also known as a lactation consultant there is a demand for women who have experienced breastfeeding to help new mothers do the same. The benefits of breastfeeding are numerous and the NHS is keen to ensure that as many mothers as possible participate.

There are very positive psychological benefits of baby bonding with mother combined with the nutritional advantages of breast milk over man-made alternatives. A mother's breast milk is not only a source of nutrition it also contains natural antibodies that help the infant fight infection. There is some evidence that these antibodies help the child throughout its life. And finally let's

not forget the obvious financial implications. Breast milk is free and if a mother breastfeeds for two years that saves an awful lot of money on milk powder.

Not all new mothers find breastfeeding easy and if they give up and move to formula milk it is impossible to go back because the body only continues to provide milk so long as it is continuously taken. If the milk is not taken by a baby the mother's body (very cleverly) assumes the milk is not required and stops supplying it so it quickly dries up. Therefore it is crucial that new mothers are given support and advice early on to help them breastfeed successfully and have the choice to continue to do so for as long as they wish.

So, if you have breastfed your baby you may be interested in helping other women do the same. First you must train to be a breastfeeding counselor with The Association of Breastfeeding Mothers. Then, after you have gained sufficient experience, you could move on to further training as a lactation consultant and charge for work in hospitals or private practice. A trained consultant can earn up to £15 per hour but this is the sort of work that could fit around a family and you will also get a lot of personal satisfaction from helping other women who were once in the same position as you.

Useful info: The NHS breastfeeding resources are at www.breastfeeding.nhs.uk and the Association of Breastfeeding Mothers is at www.abm.me.uk

Risk	
Return	££
Time	ⓟ ⓟ
Training	📖 📖 📖

9

Busking or street performing

Busking is the name given to someone who performs in the street for tips and gratuities. When you say the word busker it normally conjures up images of a crusty bloke with a beaten up guitar doing Beatle covers on the tube but you do not necessarily need tiptop music abilities to turn a few quid from entertaining the public. Although a healthy dose of courage does help, particularly when you are starting out.

Activities undertaken by buskers can include acrobatics, performing animals, balloon sculpting, card tricks, clowning, comedy, contortions and escapes, dance, fire eating, fortune-telling, juggling, magic and musical performance acts (vocal or instrumental), puppeteering, snake charming, storytelling or poetry recital, street art (sketching and painting, etc.), living statue, street theatre (including the creepy art of being a mime) or sword swallowing.

A few considerations: pick a legal site (some spots require a license); try not to block the pavement as this can cause accidents; conversely try and find a pitch where you get a good level of people traffic (particularly aim for an audience who have a bit of disposable cash like tourists or shoppers); Saturdays are best; keep a respectable distance from established buskers (it's polite); and try and enjoy yourself (punters are more likely to reward you if you are happy in your work). Also, to help those first time busker nerves remember that busking is an anonymous activity whose success depends solely on pleasing a bunch of people that don't know you and who you will never see again!

Useful info: check your local council website and contact them to see if you need a permit

Tips: talk to other buskers in the area to get the lowdown on local customs

Risk	💣
Return	£
Time	🕐-🕐🕐🕐🕐
Training	📖

10

Car booting

Aside from the money-making aspect, car boots sales are tremendous fun. Each year £1.5 billion is spent at car boot sales in the UK with one million people visiting one every weekend during the main season (Easter to November).

For many this can be a soft introduction to the world of making an extra couple of quid as this is raw commerce at its best. Selling something that you don't want and turning it into cash is an incredible thrill, even if the amounts are relatively small. And there is the excitement of finding a great bargain which you can keep for yourself, give as a gift or take it onto the next step in your program to make extra cash and resell on the internet (see eBay on page 40).

There are two distinct elements to car booting.

The Visitor. Seasoned car boot visitors will get there early and be in the queue as the doors open as the real treats are normally snapped up in the first hour. Entry to a car boot sale can be anything up to £5. Always offer low and go for bulk deals. Often offering to buy three things for one low price in amongst the confusion and heat of battle will disguise the gem that you have your eye on. If a seller won't match your price

£

£

Case Study

**Name: Michelle
Fisher
Age: 27
Occupation:
Sales
Executive**

Michelle is a busy working mum of three, but loves her money-making sideline.

I have recently returned to work after the birth of my third child but I supplement my income by finding things at carboots and then reselling them on eBay. I find most people don't want to do the hunting around but are happy to log onto the internet and purchase things. This allows traders like me to make a profit by doing the work for them.

Even if I was making lots of money in my day job I think I would still continue to do this. I love the excitement it brings me; both the bargain hunting side and the enjoyment of selling it at a higher price.

My partner and I scour carboot sales, markets and junk shops at the weekend looking for bargains. As well as making an extra bit of money I love the excitement of buying something at a low price and selling it on at a high price.

One of my best trading experiences happened quite recently. I purchased a Chloe handbag from a car boot sale for £8. Early the following week I sold it for £130 netting a healthy profit of £122 within the space of a few days.

At night when the kids are in bed I upload the things I'm selling. At this moment in time I am selling a Flymo, a mountain bike, a light sabre and an iron!

offer be prepared to walk away and come back later. Car owners always want to go home with an empty boot! That's the point.

The Car booter. Pack the car the night before and get there early to ensure you get a good pitch. A bit of forward planning will mean you arrive in a composed mental state ready to take on the hoards who want to get your goods for less than you want to sell them.

Also getting in and getting set up early gives you access to the best kept secret in car booting – the sneak preview. Experienced car booters will get their gear on display quickly and then have a bit of time to have a walk around and snap up any bargains before the general public is allowed in.

Keep your prices high to start off with. There's no point in clearing everything in the first few hours only to find you have to wait until the end to get your car out. And remember you're there to make money so be disciplined about how much stuff you buy from other car booters. Car boots are like an Aladdin's Cave so be careful you don't trade one boot full of junk for another!

Useful info: www.carbootjunction.com

Tips: I have the same advice for both the car booter and the visitor – dress warm, wear comfortable shoes, be polite (I put this in because so many people are not polite when I have been to car boots), carry lots of change, take spare carrier bags, have fun

Risk	
Return	££
Time	⏰⏰⏰
Training	📖

11
Childminder

With more and more women returning to work after having children there is a growing demand for high quality childcare. Not every woman wants her child in a nursery every day, all day, particularly if they are very young children, or their children might be of school age and only need looking after for a few hours at the end of the day or in the summer holidays. Some people will need childcare at night or at the weekend.

Childminding offers the potential to have an incredibly rewarding and responsible career with all the benefits of home-based working and a high degree of flexibility. It is also possible to care for your own children at the same time which makes it a wonderful opportunity for women with families of their own.

Childminders work in their own homes caring for other people's children with all that entails. You need to be aged at least 18 to become a child minder. You do not need any qualifications, but you do need to be registered with Ofsted (Office for Standards in Education, Children's Services and Skills) before you can look after children under the age of eight.

If you look after children up to the age of five, you will need to show that you meet the requirements of the Early Years Foundation Stage (EYFS), which sets standards for children's care, development and learning.

Your first step to becoming registered is to contact your local Children's Information Service (CIS). Once you have applied to Ofsted you will receive a home inspection and an interview to ensure you are a suitable person to care for children, have a medical check and complete both an introductory training and first aid course. You will also need clearance from the Criminal Records Bureau for yourself and anyone else in your home aged over 16.

You could get help with the costs of setting up your childminding business by applying for a childminder start-up grant. The grants are administered by local authorities' Early Years teams.

Useful info: for more details go to www.careersadvice.direct.gov.uk or the website of the National Childminding Association, www.ncma.org.uk

Tips: obviously it helps if you like children

Risk	
Return	££
Time	⏰ ⏰
Training	📖 📖

12
Children's entertainer

A word of caution here. If you don't like children move on now, do not collect your £200 and perhaps consider beer making. Watching someone play the clown may look easy but children's entertainers earn their money. Minute for minute it's harder work than coal mining. OK, I made that up (and sorry to any coalminers reading), but don't think this is an easy ride.

You carry a significant responsibility on your shoulders. Not only do you have to make the birthday child happy you also have to ensure their friends are happy. A duff children's entertainer can scar a child for life, affect their place in the school pecking order and make

them social outcasts. The side effects can make ripples in the parents' social lives and you can leave destruction in your wake. OK, I'm being dramatic. But don't take this lightly.

However, if you do love kids, have endless patience and stamina and a loud 'way about you' then this is an ideal gig to net you some extra quids. Most kid's parties are at the weekends so if you have a full-time job then fitting this in is quite possible. Expect to be able to charge between £50 and £100 for a standard party depending on where you live.

There are various ways to tackle this:

One option is the classic clown/magician combo. You'll need some basic magic skills and your local bookshop will have a number of books on their shelves to get you going. A stock supply of jokes and rudimentary balloon sculpting (again there are lots of books available on the art of balloons) will get you on your way. Practice, practice, practice. Before you put

yourself in the commercial arena try out your act on your kids or other family members if you don't have your own. The first real performance you might want to consider offering for free to get some feedback. Once you're up and running you can do some local advertising and if you are good word of mouth will spread of your new enterprise.

Another option that we recommend is to go for a franchise. There are a number of these available with different themes. For example, princesspartyz.co.uk will promote their parties and when they have a booking they would send in the franchisee local to the area – namely you. You get all the training and support as well as the products such as goody bags and cakes. Companies like these also have the advantage of being able to tap into current trends, such as High School Musical which at the time of writing is very popular and will make you well sought after.

Useful info: read *The Birthday Party Business* by Bruce Fife or take a look at www. princesspartyz.co.uk

Tips: only suitable for people who love children. Don't undertake this without doing lots of practice as the stakes are high

Risk	
Return	££
Time	🕐 🕐 🕐
Training	📖 📖 📖

13
Clean recycle bins

In the old days you put your bags out on a Thursday night so the bin men could pick them up the next morning. Foxes, cats and *News of the World* journalists would have a field day going through your rubbish trying to find lamb chop bones or incriminating evidence that you were cheating on your wife and by Friday morning the roads of Britain would be awash with rubbish.

We also threw away all sorts of useful stuff like cardboard and bottles which can be separated, shipped to Third World countries and then put in their landfill sites. NOT ANY MORE.

The wheelie bin entered our lives about ten years ago and has quickly become part of the refuse landscape. There are more than 20 million in service and like germs they continue to swarm and multiply in a variety of colours. I now have three: one for organic waste (green), one for recycling (blue) and another for general rubbish (black). There is talk of a fourth bin for computers which seem to become obsolete and thus worthless the minute you plug them in.

So there are twenty million consumer and commercial bins and growing. Anyone see an opening here? Now unlike your old tin dustbin which you simply rinse out from time to time the unwieldy nature of a wheelie bin means that you actually have to get in them to clean them properly. The result is that most aren't cleaned and end up smelling like Grimsby in a heat wave.

This is where the wheelie bin cleaning idea comes in. You will need a portable steam cleaner and some detergents and possibly a van, although we think a car with a decent-sized boot would probably do the trick. Expect to charge

£3 per standard household bin. Operators in this market are selling annual contracts of 12 cleans so you would get £36 from a client. You could build this up as a weekend business, either advertising your services with mail drops or local classifieds. This is a market that can only grow so grab it now.

Useful info: www.wheeliebin.co.uk – this company offers all the kit and training as a franchise if you don't fancy doing it all yourself from scratch although the cash outlay involved will probably mean you need to undertake this as a full-time job rather than a bit of lolly on the side

Tips: see if anyone else in the area is doing this before buying lots of kit. Remember, where there's muck there's brass!

Risk	🌑🌑
Return	££
Time	🕐🕐🕐
Training	📖📖

14
Comping and quizzing

What is a comper? Comping is the entering of free competitions such as prize draws, slogan tiebreakers and crossword puzzles in an organized and committed way. As opposed to the randomly haphazard way that most of us approach competitions (particularly after discovering that we had been ripped off by the TV companies for so long).

The competitions are usually promotions that have been created to advertise a new product or company, increase sales, increase internet traffic, collect marketing information or promote brand awareness.

And now I'm going to tell you a secret. I have been in magazine publishing for eight years and the thing that most people don't realise is that hardly anyone ever enters these competitions. We have had the most fabulous prizes offered through magazines that I have worked with and we were continuously baffled by the less than anticipated response we received.

Most people assume they will never win and subsequently don't bother. But the truth is that the odds are million times better than the National Lottery (currently about 1 in 14 million). If you enter a competition run in your small local paper (let's assume it has 25,000 readers), of those readers let's say 1% try their luck (and I can tell you that 1% is on the high side), this means that only 250 people will enter. This gives you a one in 250 chance of winning.

You should be aware that to be considered a serious comper you will need to be entering about 30 competitions per week. The internet has made the process of entering cheaper because you don't have to physically post as many entries so the cost of participation is almost nothing apart from the initial outlay for the purchase of magazines and newspapers in which to find the offers.

So what are the chances of making any serious money? Well, the answer to that question is: not great. Like any endeavor the more you put into it the more you will get out but lady luck has a big part to play. But you can stack the odds in your favour by entering as many competitions as you can get your hands on. Some compers can win hundreds of prizes over the span of their career ranging from a fistful of luncheon vouchers to cars or holidays. One comper recently won a house (although this is now sadly believed to be worth less than the price of the newspaper they purchased in which they found the competition).

Useful info: www.winningcompetitions.co.uk and www.compersgrapevine.co.uk

Tips: don't ever hand over your credit card or bank details – if you are asked, it's a scam. Join a local compers society to swap tips and notes

Risk	💣
Return	£
Time	⏱⏱⏱
Training	📖

15
Concert and events staff

When rock bands tour the country they normally have a large entourage supporting them. From roadies to personal trainers to accountants they are like an army on the move. However, when they roll into your town they also create a huge demand for casual labour. When you go to a concert think about all the casual staff around you, from the angry guy in the high visibility tabard barking into a walkie-talkie to the spotty youth who serves you one of those burgers made out of sawdust and bits of meat they're not allowed to give pets for which they charge you £8. By its nature a lot of this work can be done in the evenings so fits in with other work commitments.

Usually you will become a temporary employee and the amount of work can vary according to the size and number of events taking place and the hours of work and how regular it is. Once registered, individuals are then contacted and offered specific periods of work in advance on a shift basis. One of the key character traits for this sort of work will be reliability and if you prove that you can turn up on time for your shift then you should be able to build up a good level of part-time work.

The types of positions include Kitchen Porters, Glass Collectors, Kiosk Assistants, Cashiers, Bar Staff, Foodsnack Assistants, Silver Service Waiting Staff, Wine Staff, Food Service and Food Preparation Assistants, Cooks/Chefs, Furniture Porters.

Concerts and events also need high levels of security and in most venues of significance there will be a large requirement for temporary security staff, traffic officers and concert stewards. You should be over 18 to consider the security positions and should be able to provide references.

Rates for these sorts of jobs aren't brilliant and in most instances you will be looking at pay rates around the minimum wage. On the plus side it can be very sociable with lots of other staff in a similar boat and if you like live music or big sporting events then you get to watch them for free. Most venues whether they be exhibition halls, concert halls or sporting venues, will have a website with full details on how you can register to work there.

Tips: have a good set of references typed up and ready to hand in with your application. As with many of these standing around sort of jobs comfortable shoes and warm undergarments will come in handy towards the end of a night

Risk	💣
Return	£
Time	⏱⏱
Training	📖📖

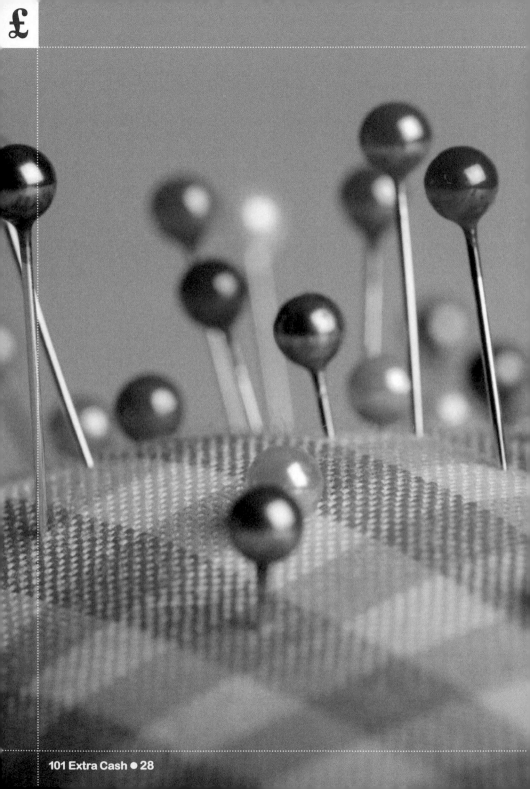

£

16
Crafting

Do you have a little creative streak? If you do then why not try your hand at making things and then selling them. On paper it sounds hard but read the inspiring case study on the next page to see how one mum set up her own jewellery company from scratch. Over the past few years handmade crafts have become more desirable as people have come to value and appreciate unique items that have been made with care (rather than the mass produced plastic rubbish that is imported from Asia that my kids seem to get lots of each Christmas).

Before trying to sell your own work visit a few craft shows. This will enable you to see the quality and range of the work being sold by others and may give you some ideas of what you can make. It will also, crucially, give you an indication of the price point that you could sell your goods for.

Once you've made the decision about what you can make it's time to source the component parts. Most towns have some sort of crafting shop and it can be useful to go along, have a browse and see what the prices are. You should then check these prices on the internet to see if you can get them cheaper. Cost control is everything here as although it's rewarding to make crafts you are here to make money out of them. We don't recommend buying in bulk to start off just in case you find that you don't really like making necklaces and your spare room now contains three million crystal beads. But once you are confident and have made some sales then bulk buying will save you money in the long run.

Market research is key. Talk to your friends and family about the sort of things they would like to buy and try and cater to a local market as these people are likely to be your first customers. There are several ways that you can sell your products. Firstly, as we have mentioned [where?], there is the subtle and almost cost free way of getting your new scheme off the ground and that is to invite friends and family around for a coffee morning (your cost of going to market being some coffee and a packet of biscuits). Tell them that you are testing your products on them. You are guaranteed to make sales this way and this can be a great way to gauge opinion and also shift your first batch of stock.

The other most effective way of selling handcrafted goods is through craft fairs. Be careful to put together your business strategy. Work out how many units you have to sell to break even and if the costs are too high in relation to your price point then don't do it. If the stall is going to cost £100 per day and you are selling items at £15 with a £10 margin then you only need to sell 10 to break even. Some craft fairs will charge a percentage on what is sold which can be a lower risk way of entering the market.

You can also sell your goods at wholesale to local retailers who already have an existing customer base. The internet also provides an obvious route to market but this can be expensive if you are thinking of creating your own site. In the first instance we would suggest using eBay (see page 40) to test the water.

Useful info: find your local craft fair at www.ukcraftfairs.com and for craft supplies visit www.craftingdirect.com

Tips: try and make items that interest you. You are going to be more passionate about them which will enable you to sell them more effectively plus you will enjoy making them more

Risk	🔥
Return	££
Time	⏰⏰⏰
Training	📖📖

£ Case Study

Name: Caroline Craven
Age: 30
Occupation: Full-time mum

Caroline Craven launched www.cravenand white.com in late 2008, but the inspirational journey to setting up her own money-making enterprise began many years ago.

I come from a very creative family; my father and several generations before him were photographers and my mum can turn her hand to anything – making curtains, painting or creating nativity play costumes at a moment's notice.

Like many 'creatives' I was never particularly academic at school but excelled at art. After my A levels I studied for a degree in textiles at university and I graduated in 2000 with a good degree. But then I turned my back on the creative world and eventually fell into marketing.

I got married in 2002 and quickly had two children and so I settled into life as a housewife. I really did enjoy the children when they were little but at the back of my mind I still felt I needed to do something for myself, so when the children had gone to bed I would get the sewing machine out and make a whole array of craft items and, having told my friends, about this I would often be asked to do their curtains and blinds. At last I had a use other than just pureeing vegetables and wiping bottoms!

A friend of mine suggested selling some of my creations and I dismissed it thinking she was just being kind. However, she continued to talk about it and eventually persuaded me to come to her house one evening when she had invited some friends around.

I remember being so nervous – what if they didn't like it or, even worse, if they laughed at my work. To my complete amazement they loved it and were soon sitting there with armfuls of bits and pieces waiting to pay. I was so unprepared for the response that I didn't even have change or a cash tin. Afterwards some of the girls were asking if I would do parties for them at their houses and they were making orders for extra items that had sold out.

After they had gone I counted my evening's takings and it was the key moment that I realised that there was some money to be made from this. It was only a week till my next party booking and so the production activity had to speed up. Even my mum was getting roped in to help make up stock so I could complete the bespoke orders from the previous party.

The next party came and more bookings with it and one of the women was involved in organising charity events so put me on her list of stall holders. I just needed to work out which products were the most cost effective to make and which sold best and concentrate on producing more of these.

I began making simple jewellery and these items sold extremely well so I made more of these items. I also wanted to provide a better quality of products and so I did an evening course in silversmithing at the local college. This helped me source new suppliers which has made a huge difference to my purchasing decisions and also the quality of my materials.

My youngest child is now in nursery education which has freed up a lot of time during the day and as well as the parties I have also expanded into supplying some local retailers. I also launched my website recently and that has got off to a great start. It was well worth all the hard work and now I'm looking forward to slowly building up the business which still gives me time to run the house and be there for the kids when they come home from school.

101 Extra Cash ● 30

17
Credit card cashback

Remember one thing before you even consider this option: credit cards are dangerous. I am often dismayed at the amount of interest that some credit card companies are allowed to charge yet still be called legal. It is the worst posslble way to borrow money (other than from Big Al, the loan shark who lives next to the chippy) and my advice to you is that if you make any money from reading this book use the first slew of funds to pay off the outstanding balance as soon as you can. However, if you have credit cards with a zero balance it is actually possible to use them to your advantage and even make money from them.

Most cards give you interest free credit for between 46 and 59 days. This is the time between the point you purchase the product and the time the credit card company require you to pay for it. If you pay off all your balance you have used their money to pay for something for up to 59 days while your money stays in your bank account earning interest. OK, interest rates are pretty low at the moment so the actual money you make is not exactly significant but it's a start.

Many cards now, such as American Express, will give you cash back on what you spend. The credit card companies charge the retailers for each transaction. This can be anything up to 5% depending on the retailer concerned and their turnover with the card companies. These cash back schemes will kick back a percentage of each sale to the card holder as a loyalty bonus so it's effectively a rebate from the retailer through the card company. If you put all your household expenditure through your card for a whole year

and make sure you pay off the balance each month then you will actually make money. Work out what 1% of your household expenses are per year and see if it's worth it.

Useful info: www.moneysavingexpert.com

Tips: you have to be very organised to play the credit card game. One late payment can take you from a positive cash position to a loss. Only do this if you have zero balances

Risk	
Return	£
Time	⏲
Training	📖 📖

18
Cutting lawns

This is a great stop-gap because of its seasonal nature and has to be one of the most satisfying jobs – quick and easy with fabulous results. You'll need the right tools, though, and the crème de la crème of mowers is considered to be the petrol mower with a roller. It gives those lovely stripes and isn't a difficult mower to maintain – they sell from between £200–£4000.

Lawns need weekly mowing from May to September, and it's best to keep the grass to a height of between 2.5cm–4cm long in the summer months to give a lush look. Unless you want to be lugging the mower around the streets from job to job, you'll need to ensure you can get it in your car along with the other tools you may need. To even up lawn edges and to give a professional finish you'll need a half-moon cutter, and to rake up leaves, you'll want a light rake.

You could take it one step further and

tackle weeds, moss and patches, too, so buy a weedkiller product and lawn seed and set to work making your customers' lawns their pride and joy. If the lawn looks yellow, you could also apply a lawn feed.

When using electric mowers, keep a keen eye on the lead and ensure you have comprehensive insurance in place in case you accidentally cause any damage. You'll need gloves, hat, eye protection, a broom, rubbish sacks (you'll be expected to take the cuttings away) and sturdy footwear.

After a job, leave yourself some time to put flyers through the neighbours' doors to promote your business: no doubt you've been watched working and the word has spread that you're in the area. You can negotiate fees with each customer, depending on the size of the garden and the state of the grass, but most gardeners will charge from around £30.

Useful info: www.lawn.co.uk, www.gardeningdata.co.uk and www.gardenersworld.com

Tips: protect yourself against sunburn and insect bites. Cut your own lawn and your neighbours' to practise getting it perfect

Risk	💣
Return	££
Time	🕐🕐🕐
Training	📖

19
Dating agency

There is so much opportunity available in the dating industry. Despite the gloomy times in which we are currently living people still want

romance. Indeed, they probably want romance more than ever before.

The dating industry is split into two distinct arenas. Online dating and offline dating.

The global online dating and matchmaking industry is estimated to have grown from $40 billion in 2001 to $600 billion in 2008. And it shows no sign of slowing. This market is still open to small players and should be considered, particularly if you have a technical bent.

Before you gasp at the enormous task of building your own dating website engine and recruiting the many thousands of members required to make a site work there is a short cut. And it's called Whitelabeldating.com. The business works by pooling members. So in the central pool there are millions of members and each dating site has a separate brand or 'front end' which is the gateway to the pool. As the owner of your respective website you are responsible for promoting your own brand and you will get a hefty share of the revenue that each of your members generates for white label dating from their subscription fees. The advantage of this is that you can start a dating site tomorrow without having to spend millions of pounds marketing it nor creating the costly infrastructure behind it.

Whitelabeldating.com will pay you every two weeks for the members you sign up. You will need to spend money with a web designer on developing the look and feel of your site and if you want to make a decent amount of money then you will need to invest in advertising on the search engine networks such as Google and Yahoo. Whitelabeldating have many partners who started out as small players and who now generate many thousands of pounds per month. You can outsource the search engine marketing to a third party company and the business will only require monitoring for half an hour each day.

For the luddites among you there are still spoils to be had from this sector. Traditional matchmaking services still exist but these are hard to set up in your spare time and they require time and investment. One way of quickly building your business is to run a speed dating night.

Useful info: www.originaldating.com/contact. htm, Whitelabeldating.com

Tips: if you are married or attached make sure you tell your partner as they may think you are up to no good if you start getting dating related emails and post!

Risk	🌑🌑🌑
Return	££££
Time	🕐🕐
Training	📖📖

20
Decorating

The tiling in your bathroom looks great, the wallpapering in your lounge is superb and the paintwork in your bedrooms has a perfect finish – so could your decorating skills at home be turned into a money spinner? Quite possibly. The basic skills that any decorator needs to have, according to the City & Guilds Institute, are painting a window frame, roller application of emulsion and oil-based paint and wallpapering. Followed by refitting a radiator and different paint techniques, like spraying and glazing.

You'll also need all the equipment, like ladders, sanding equipment, rollers, paintbrushes, dustsheets, not forgetting safety equipment like safety goggles, face mask and gloves – and a big enough car or van to transport them. You will also need to investigate your insurance options and seek affiliation with a trade website to boost your new business. However, you'll need a few years' experience, references and basic qualifications to be accepted into professional organisations, such as the Painters and Decorators Association, but worth a try.

One downside to decorating as a job rather than as a weekend pursuit is that your exposure to the chemicals in oil-based paints and paint strippers is radically increased, so if you start to feel high when you're up the ladder, take a break and keep your working area well ventilated.

The decorating business is extremely competitive, and you may find you're asked to quote for jobs and hear nothing more, as most potential customers want three or more quotes before they settle on a decorator. Nonetheless, if you're personable and trustworthy, this may count for more than your price or skills, as customers want to feel at ease with a decorator in their home.

If your decorating skills are a little rusty, then take heart; many of the

well-known DIY stores have advice on their websites, so you could always print out a few and practice techniques at home. Make space in your shed or garage to store your tools and equipment tidily and to make them easily accessible, plus an area to dry out paintbrushes and rollers.

Useful info: for courses, look at www.cityandguilds.com, and for advice go to www.paintquality.co.uk and www.wickes.co.uk

Tips: get fit – it's physical work and you'll be amazed at how your muscles ache

Risk	
Return	£££
Time	⊙ ⊙ ⊙
Training	📖 📖 📖

21
Delivering pizza and fast food

Although not immediately appealing, this type of work is perfect if you're having to juggle a few different jobs, because the hours are usually 5pm till around 1am. It goes without saying that few qualifications are necessary for this work, but a clean driving licence is essential and good local knowledge of the area is an added bonus.

Depending on the food outlet you're working for, you may be provided with a car or scooter, so remember to check your employer's insurance details – you want to be covered if you're caught up in a road accident en route to a delivery address (rushing to an address to ensure the food is piping hot can be dangerous).

Drawbacks include trying to find addresses in the middle of the night, bad weather, customers who are not in and those who refuse to pay. Be street-savvy in terms of your personal safety because you will be carrying money. Always take along a mobile phone with which to call the police or to alert the fast food outlet you're working for of dangerous areas or addresses. Dealing with drunk, rude and hungry customers is also an occupational hazard, but one that can be dealt with in a polite and discreet manner to maximise any tips that might come your way.

If you're using your own car, you'll need to tell your insurance company – fully comp with liability and legal protection is your best bet. Perks of the job include free food at the end of your shift (thus reducing your supermarket bills and a great way to fill up your freezer) and flexible full-time and part-time contracts.

You can download application forms for the major pizza chains to apply for delivery jobs, while dropping into your local fast-food outlet with your CV and driving license is also an option.

Useful info: if you think this is an ideal job, then visit www.findextrawork.co.uk, www.careersatpizzahut.co.uk and www.dominos.co.uk

Tips: invest in warm clothing, practise your customer-friendly banter and brush up on your driving skills

Risk	
Return	££
Time	🕐 🕐
Training	📖

22
Dog walking

What could be better than lots of fresh air, plenty of exercise and getting paid for walking someone else's dog? If you are fit and adore dogs, then setting up your own dog-walking business makes sense. The going rate is around £10 for a half-hour walk, but you can negotiate your own fees. Potential customers will probably want to see a police check and references, while it's also a good idea to get public liability insurance.

If you feel confident, you can probably take two or three dogs for a walk at the same time, depending on the nature of the dogs and whether they are male or female.

Most dog walkers have a service agreement with their customers to ensure legal protection if the dog is injured while in their care and it also sets out the standard of care that they offer. For example, you may want to state what happens in an emergency, listing the vet's contact details if the dog is injured or if the dog causes harm or damage. You will also need the owners to stipulate that the dog is vaccinated and healthy. A visit to your solicitor will be necessary for legal advice.

You will need to invest in a pooper scooper and plastic bags to clean up after the dogs and a range of small toys with which to play 'fetch' and so on. A few spare leads won't go amiss, along with a few doggie treats to ensure obedience.

Advertising your business to maximise your customer base can be achieved by registering your service on pet directory websites, which are generally free. Nonetheless, nothing beats word-of-mouth recommendation, so get started with a few neighbours' dogs and ask the owners to recommend you to their friends.

Useful info: check out the following websites for ideas to get you started: www.ukpetsitters.com, www.dogwalkersuk.com, www.nspca.org.uk

Tips: have a water-tight service agreement in place, get chatting to dog owners in the park and practise your doggy commands. Sit!

Risk	💣
Return	££
Time	🕐🕐🕐
Training	📖

23
Domestic pet breeding

On the face of it pet breeding looks pretty easy. I mean, you buy a female pedigree dog for £600,

you do a stud deal with an owner of a male dog and a few months later you have eight puppies. The stud owner gets the pick of the bunch and then you sell the other seven for £600 each netting you a crafty four grand and you get to play with some puppies. WRONG.

Your dog will need to be properly exercised, given a good diet and will need vet treatment through its pregnancy. Then you have to think of what happens if things go wrong, like your dog needs a c-section (very expensive) or rejects the pups (harrowing) or the new owners return the pups because they've decided that they're not dog people (really annoying). Go into this with immense caution. A profitable breeding program can take 15–20 years to develop.

However, if you love dogs and have a responsible attitude there is no reason why becoming a one off dog breeder cannot be a wonderfully rewarding experience and there is a possibility that you might make some extra money on the side but, if done properly, not very much. But don't assume that your pooch can become a cash cow because it probably won't. Breeders tend to take a dim view of one-timers but since the dog has been at man's side for at least the past 15,000 years there's no reason why you should not try the experience yourself.

You can also try your hand at other less time consuming breeding such as fish (Carp) or lizards (Chameleons). Cat breeding can also be quite lucrative.

Useful info: *Successful Dog Breeding* by Chris Walkowicz and Bonnie Wilcox

Tips: if you don't think you can handle the responsibility that comes with dog breeding then why not try breeding carp

Risk

Return ££

Time ⊕⊕⊕⊕
Training 📖📖

24
Drug testing

This money-making scheme has had some bad press recently when in early 2006 six young men were given what was thought a routine drug test only to find their heads swelled up to twice the normal size and their immune systems were destroyed. One of them had to have his legs amputated after most of his organs shut down.

To the men it seemed like a good deal when it was first offered. Two grand to take a drug and then put your feet up and drink some tea for a few days while they had some tests done to them. Instead they endured days of agony and had their lives stripped away from them. So one might conclude that this is a bit of a duff way of netting a bit of extra coin.

The truth of it is that the six young men and the multimillion pound lawsuit that ensued (the main company went bust in the end) has probably meant even stricter guidelines on drug testing. Also you can choose to participate in tests that seem less risky such as how cigarettes affect you (not so bad if you are a smoker). The sort of testing ranges from being given a common cold to administration of cancer drugs.

If you don't like being prodded and poked and having needles stuck in you then this probably isn't for you. On the plus side as well as getting paid you often get to stay for a few nights and generally get fed and pampered (apart from the needles). Rates can range from £50 a day right up to a few thousand pounds for more risky tests that involve a degree of 'pain' and go on for some time.

This would not suit someone with a full-time job or kids to look after and has traditionally been the preserve of students and hard-up artists (film director Robert Rodriguez famously used funds earned from doing drugs trials to make his 1991 film *Bedhead*).

For further information check university notice boards or use a search engine to determine test companies in your local area. Typically to qualify you must be over 18, in good health, registered with a doctor for more than three years (who holds three years' medical history) and not using regular medication that would interfere with the drug trial.

Useful info: www.testwiththebest.com

Tips: don't tell your mother

Risk	🎆🎆🎆🎆🎆
Return	££
Time	⏰⏰⏰
Training	zero

25
eBay

This really should have been number one but we're doing it alphabetically so it didn't fit. Entire books have been written about how to trade on eBay and we've only got 400 words so it's hard to do it justice but this is our favourite.

What started out in 1995 as the Echo Bay Technology Group (first item sold was a broken laser pointer) is now one of the global giants of the internet. It defines what the internet is so good at doing. Connecting people. Finding the one person in the world who wants to sell the former car (a VW Golf) of the current Pope and connecting him to the Golden Palace online casino who purchased it for $277,000 dollars last year.

Ordinary people from all walks of life make money on eBay all the time. From housewives to students, to business people to pensioners, they all use eBay to make a bit of money. Some people make a full time career out of it, others do it as a hobby. I know of a city banker who earns hundreds of thousands a year in his day job but who trades in Dr Who memorabilia on eBay in his spare time. The earnings are a fraction of what he makes from selling dodgy financial packages to my granddad's pension plan but the thrill of buying something and then selling it for a profit is almost addictive.

If you have not ventured onto eBay yet I would suggest you start out by making some purchases to see how the system works. It is very straightforward and once you've found your feet then you can dip your toe in the water and try and sell something that you own that you don't want any more. My first sale was a vintage bicycle that I had bought my wife from a local market in London (she said it was rubbish) and I sold it for £120 and made £30.

Once you have got the hang of it you can then start to speculate a little bit and perhaps pick up things from your local charity shop, tip shop (many tips these days have a shop where they rescue items that can be sold) and car boot sales.

Experienced eBayers will use resource sites such as esources.co.uk which helps traders source goods in bulk from all over the world.

Useful info: *eBay.co.uk for Dummies* and www.esources.co.uk

Tips: avoid scammers by never dealing directly with a buyer. Always go through the eBay system and try and buy from people that have a good eBay history (see the star system). Don't buy in bulk until you are confident of the process and market

Risk	
Return	£-£££
Time	🕐-🕐🕐🕐
Training	📖

26
Envelope stuffing

We've put this one in as a bit of a warning as everyone seems to have heard about making money from stuffing envelopes and this came up several times in the course of putting this guide together. But in all the research we have done we have yet to find anyone that has actually turned a profit doing this job.

You've seen the small ads and you've always wondered... can I make a small fortune by stuffing envelopes? The short answer seems to be no. It's a scam and has in the past been an extremely successful one. You end up out of pocket, with no recourse and a great deal of frustration. Get wise and resist the urge to explore it further. Most of these disreputable companies ask you to make a payment upfront, a registration fee if you like, then they send you the envelopes, the literature that goes into the envelopes and address labels. They will send you very specific instructions as to how stuff the envelopes, position the label and so on, and then you return the unsealed envelopes to the company, to be checked that the envelopes meet their 'criteria'.

It doesn't take much imagination to realise that at this point, your stuffing skills will fall short and they will deem your work unsatisfactory, even if you have followed the instructions to the letter. You won't get paid and your 'registration' fee is non-refundable. You would also have bought the stamps for the envelopes and paid for them to be returned to the company. On some occasions, envelope stuffing companies have been known to simply bank your cheque and never contact you again.

Take a look at www.workfromhome phenomena.co.uk and www.thriftyfun.com for a more detailed account. Bearing all this in mind, you may still feel that there is a work opportunity out there like this – and maybe there is. Small local companies may well need help in this area particularly at a time when they have laid off staff to reduce costs, and you could target them directly with a proposal and rates for home office assistance, but guard against advertising as a stuffing envelope business if you want to retain any professional integrity.

Tips: don't even go there – you will lose money

Risk	💣💣💣💣💣💣
Return	zero
Time	🕐🕐🕐🕐
Training	zero

27
Escorting

Although escorting is an option available to both sexes the end result is usually quite different.

For women there is a fine line between being an escort and charging somebody for an hour or two of your sparkling company and being an escort and charging someone for a couple of hours of hanky panky. Unfortunately if you go down this path the chances are that you would up engaging in the latter and although the money can be good the personal price you pay is something that's likely to be with you for ever. Think what you are selling? To this end we don't really encourage female escorting and would advise against it.

For men the idea of being paid to put on a dinner suit, be taken out for dinner and then have sex with your client at the end of the night is like Christmas and New Year rolled into one with a magnum of champagne on top. The truth is it rarely happens like that.

Women who are prepared to pay for the company of a cultured, educated, engaging and dashingly handsome companion expect top drawer specimens of manhood. These kind of men are few and far between and in all likelihood the fact that you are reading a book called *101 Ways to Make a Bit of Extra Cash in a Recession* probably means that you are not this kind of man. It ain't gonna happen my friend!

It has become more socially acceptable for women to pay for sex but our research indicates that the demand for such a service is very small and you are unlikely to make an extra income from it. Shame though. That would have been a good one!

Useful info: for men, www.scarletmagazine. co.uk has a classified section where women seek male escorts

Risk	⦿⦿⦿
Return	££
Time	⏱⏱⏱
Training	**zero**

28
Extra

You love films and television drama, without question, but could you turn this lifelong passion into a quick money-earner? Quite possibly if you consider taking on the role of an extra. These non-speaking parts are well paid and interesting. What's more, you may discover hidden acting talents you never thought you had when practising a brooding presence or a coy glance.

You don't need any qualifications or previous experience and there is no upper or lower age limit. Working as an extra means you will be guaranteed a minimum wage for the work you do by the unions Equity and Bectu. For example a day's work at the BBC is around £60, with overtime payments of around £10 an hour – and you will get free meals, too.

If you fancy brushing shoulders with celebrities, adding to the ambience of a film or TV drama and exploring your own acting talents, then you have nothing to lose. The tricky part comes when trying to choose an extras agency with which to register to ensure you get the pick of the jobs. Casting directors approach agencies for the extras they need, so this is where you need to choose carefully.

Most agencies ask you to register online and create a profile, and charges to do this vary. Some may ask for a membership fee of around £25 for a

£

year, while others charge what's called a 'hosting' fee of around £10 where your CV and photo are held online. Often film and TV shoots start early, around 7am and can continue late, so between takes there is a lot of hanging around and you may find your initial enthusiasm for the film set wanes.

Useful info: visit www.extras.co.uk, www.universalextras.co.uk , www.equity.org.uk for more information

Tips: create an outstanding personal profile online, research agencies and be prepared to wait a while for the work to come

Risk	
Return	££
Time	☺ ☺ ☺
Training	📖

29
Fashion

If fashion is your passion then there is money to be made, turning what has been a drain on your expenses up to now into a positive money spinner.

The first step is to stop hoarding. Go through your closet and take a good look at what you actually wear and weed out the sad little items that have been hanging in the dark for the past couple of years because they don't fit or you never actually liked them after you'd bought them. These clothes, shoes and accessories should be off giving pleasure to someone else – and they can make you some money at the same time.

EBay is still the best portal for turning your trash into someone else's treasure. It is simple to

list your items and, as you will know if you've ever searched on it yourself, it is amazing what people put up there and what people actually buy. Another interesting website is www.fashionspace.com where it is possible to buy, sell or swap your independently designed, vintage or second-hand fashion.

Vintage is very hot. It seems strange that just a few short years ago we would have looked funny at anyone wearing second-hand clothes. Surely that was the preserve of grungy students? Now it is the quickest way to stand apart from the crowd as there is no chance you will turn up at a party and find someone else wearing the same dress as you. To make it even more acceptable we termed it 'vintage'.

Check out your mother's – or even better – your grandmother's loft. Scour charity shops for gems – Oxfam even has a website now (www.oxfam.org.uk). Car boots and antique centres or fairs are also a good source – it is not always the case that the stallholders know the value of what they have. Everyone knows their Chanel, YSL and Dior, but do your research so that you can recognise the less well known designers of the past that can command exorbitant prices.

Tip: you actually have to sell your finds and not just keep them for yourself!

Risk	
Return	£
Time	☺ ☺
Training	zero

30
Find a friend a job

This is a strange one but it does work. Zubka.

com is a job referral website where you can earn good money by recommending friends for jobs. If there is a job posted on Zubka and you think it is right for someone you know then you can refer them for the job. This really can be anyone you know from family members (no matter how distant), to old school chums to work colleagues – as long as they are perfect for that job. And if they do get the job then you make some money.

For example, the money you get for placing someone in a £50K job is £3600. And the beauty of this is that its not just about the money, you get a warm fuzzy feeling for helping out someone you know. If you're a sociable person with lots of contacts this could be a great way to make an extra coupe of quid.

Useful info: www.zubka.com

Risk	
Return	£
Time	
Training	

31
Fishing and hunting

If you feel the call of the great outdoors and want to put your hunting and fishing skills to the test, you could earn a tidy sum. It goes without saying that different types of fishing require different rods, tackle and bait, whether you choose the sea or the river, and can prove an expensive investment, so look for second-hand bargains.

There is a great deal of regulation, rightly so, to protect fish stocks, so read up on the Environment Agency website for all the necessary information you might need, www.environment-agency.gov.uk. The fishing season runs from April to March and a licence costs around £68, available from your local post office (if you still have such a thing near you). Don't neglect to buy this as the penalty can be anything up to £2500 and getting a hefty fine before you earn any extra pie 'n' mash isn't really in the spirit of this book.

Top-price catches are salmon and halibut (the latter being a deep sea catch and difficult to fit in after the school run).

As for hunting, you may find that shooting duck, pheasant, rabbit and wild boar reaps benefits. Often considered a sport for the very rich and famous, hunting has become increasingly popular. You'll need a firearms certificate for your weapon (the police also need to know you have a gun) and be aware of the legal game seasons (which vary depending on what you're hunting).

The difficulty you may encounter is actually finding a shoot locally that you can join and which is affordable. Check out www.hotbarrels.com for shoots and www.shootinguk.co.uk, www.sportinggun.co.uk and www.thefield.co.uk for information. Pheasant shooting costs about £25 a bird (a 200-bird day for eight guns will cost about £5000), while wood-pigeon and wild fowl clubs charge much less.

Fish and meat merchants and farms may buy what you've caught or shot, so look online at a directory website like www.ukfoodonline.co.uk for those local to you and approach them direct. If you shot a wild boar for instance, this sells for £7.50 per kilo and boars weigh around 60–70 kg, so you're looking at around £500. Fish merchants will buy whole salmon from between £7–12 per kilo, while trout is around £1 per kilo and halibut is £9 per kilo: visit www.fishupdates.com for current prices.

Tips: make sure you have the right licenses

Tips: it's never as easy as it looks and be prepared for the fact that you might be a lousy shot. Don't wander around killing ducks and trying to sell them as they are probably owned by someone and that would be classed as theft

Risk	🎇🎇
Return	£
Time	🕐🕐🕐
Training	📖📖

32
Flower arranging

Make the most of your green-fingers and create stunning arrangements. If you have an abundance of flowers in your garden, that's great, but don't forget to check out your local market and if possible your nearest flower market for good deals and the very best blooms for your displays. They

trade early in the morning; for example, New Covent Garden market in London opens from 3am to 11am. And for those of you who think this is just seasonal work, think again, as winter wreaths, birthdays, anniversaries, Valentine's Day and Mother's Day mean there's always an opportunity to sell flowers.

For inspiration and to learn more skills, consider a home study course in floral arrangements with the National Association of Flower Arrangement Societies. You can become an affiliated member of this society (it has 70,000 members) for just £35 a year – great on your CV. The course gives you a basic grounding in flower arranging and design techniques.

To sell your flower arrangements and hanging baskets, seek out a market stall rental, the cost of which varies, but can be anything from around £50 a day. In most cases, you will have to join a waiting list for a pitch. Otherwise, set up shop outside your own house (check out your local authority guidelines on street trading) and go to car boot sales, craft fairs and so on.

To promote your skills, you could also give bouquets and arrangements to local hospitals, schools and cafes, with your details tucked inside. A big-name florist like Interflora will charge from around £20 for an expertly arranged bouquet or basket, so price yours competitively with this in mind. Visit discount shops for cheap buckets in which to store your blooms and cellopane, ribbon and floristy wire.

Useful info: for more details on flower arrangement societies visit www.nafas.org.uk. For bargain supplies and tips, go to www.easyfloristsupplies.co.uk and www.smithers oasis.com

Tips: be confident and scour the countryside for twigs, leaves and ferns that will add an extra twist to your arrangements

Risk	
Return	££
Time	🕐 🕐 🕐
Training	📖 📖

33
Focus groups

The massive cost of rolling out new national brands or products means that most big companies undertake some kind of research to determine whether there is a demand for their exciting new development. This can be for food and drink, cleaning products, perfumes, toiletries, financial services, magazines or even the endings to Hollywood blockbusters.

To bring a product to a national market costs millions and millions of pounds. When you consider that the average new magazine launch budget is now over ten million pounds the stakes are so high that it's plainly worth investing a few thousand in the early days to ensure its going to be wanted by the audience it's designed to reach. Many products and ideas have not got off the drawing board as a result of poor focus group response. Similarly if a brand has lost its way this is a very effective method of finding out what the owner needs to do to readjust to consumer expectations (you think someone would have done this with Woolies!).

So how do you make money out of it?

Focus groups are usually organised by a company at a venue of their choice where the physical goods or products can be displayed or you can watch them on film. Often the companies are interested in how a group reacts to a particular idea and you will be expected to give your opinion with the other people in the room present and often discussions will take place which might give a deeper understanding.

You will typically be matched up to ten similar types of people who would relate to the product or brand in question. If a video game company was testing a new war game format then they are unlikely to want to have a 70-year-old retired tea lady on their panel and would probably seek young men with disposable income who like fighting games and gore. Similarly if a company was bringing out a new kind of doily then they would be seeking the valued opinion of 70-year-old retired tea ladies. You get the general drift of this.

So you register your details with a company and they will keep you on file until an appropriate group comes up. You can expect to get paid anything from £20 to £100 depending on the location and time. Some years ago I went to a focus group for an exciting new art company that was forming and as well as £50 cash we also got given free wine (and the evening ended in a very heated debate about modern art and was it rubbish). I also attended a focus group at Tussauds Group and was fed, given some fine wine, paid to attend and also got free tickets to Chessington World of Adventures.

Useful info: www.insightfocusgroups.co.uk and www.qualityeye.com

Tips: if a focus group asks you to pay to register you are being ripped off. So don't hand over money. Register with as many sites as you can as the more you are on file the more you are likely to get chosen

Risk	💣
Return	££
Time	🕐 🕐
Training	**zero**

34
Foraging

Here's an interesting fact. Although you would think living in the Stone Age was particularly awful without your central heating or hair straighteners the truth is that your distant ancestors didn't work nearly as hard as you. Many ancient historians and anthropological experts think that ancient man worked for only a few hours a day.

Humans as we know them have been more or less the same for the past 200,000 years. The modern notion of an asset collecting, control freaking humanity has been in place for about 6000 years. Go back beyond those 6000 years and you will discover that our needs were remarkably simple. Food and shelter. With only two main things to really concern ourselves with it left a lot of time for lying around not really doing much. The time that was not spent lounging would have been spent hunting things or foraging for edible roots, nuts, fruits and plants. So foraging is actually one of the most natural and ancient of human activities.

I find it hard to explain how satisfying it is in September that I can step outside my kitchen and pluck an apple from my little apple tree and eat it. Or walk in the local park and pick blackberries. There is nothing as pure as self-sufficiency and one of the disappointments I have about our modern world is that we have lost all contact with what has been so important to us for most of our history.

Food For Free by Richard Mabey is a delightful and fascinating handbook which pretty much does what is says on the cover. It lists in detail many foods that can be found all around us that simply require you to find them and then eat them. There are also helpful hints and recipes to turn the foods into something more interesting. I tried making the dandelion root coffee, for example, and remarkably it tastes distinctly coffee-ish (not that I think that Starbucks has much to worry about, I must say) and is very easy to make. And my garden is full of dandelions!

I have to be honest at this point and declare that making substantial money from what grows around is not easy unless by accident of geography you live near to areas where certain desirable funguses grow. British Summer Truffles (Tuber aestivum) grow wild all over the country and fetch about £300 per lb. Interestingly the last few wet summers have significantly increased the harvest and there are more truffles around than usual.

Their value is in their rarity so you're unlikely to stumble across them in your local park but if you are interested in developing this further then get a copy of *Truffles* by Elisabeth Luard. Brambles which produce blackberries are also prolific in this country, although you are unlikely to be able to sell these in their freshly picked state but, by adding value, such as making them into a pie, may enable you to sell them to a local deli or at a fête or country fayre.

Useful info: www.wildmanwildfood.com, www.goselfsufficient.co.uk, *Food For Free* by Richard Mabey, *Truffles* by Elisabeth Luard.

Tips: don't forage on private land (you'll be guilty of the double crime of trespassing and theft!). Foraging is more bountiful in the summer months. Many plants are poisonous so don't eat anything until you check a reference book

Risk	💣※
Return	£
Time	🕐
Training	📖

35
Fossiling

Whole books exists on fossil hunting and I would recommend you buy one if you wish to pursue this as a money-making activity because we cannot give the topic full justice in this guide. However, this can be quite lucrative if you have time on your hands to go and hunt for fossils.

Fossils exist everywhere but for first timers trying this out you need to be able to find them easily (chances are you're going to have to go very deep in your garden to find anything of note – although my son recently brought home a Devil's Toenail, or Gryphaea, a Jurassic oyster which he found in his school playground, evidence that 200 million years ago Warwickshire was covered by a shallow sea).

The most accessible and easy to extract fossils exist throughout the country in areas of sedimentary rock that are exposed. Sedimentary is the kind of rock that has been built up on the floor of a lake or sea. It is built up of trillions of microscopic items of debris (or sediment) that falls to the ocean floor and then gets squeezed together under pressure from the further debris that falls on top of it. Eventually it forms rock. Anything that falls onto the seabed gets encased in the rock as it develops and the soft tissue of the creature eventually turns to rock leaving an impression.

Limestone is a sedimentary rock that is widespread throughout the country and the best places to search are on the coast where the sea routinely bashes up the coastline revealing rich seams of fossils. After big storms can be a particularly fruitful time to search. Limestone is a crumbly stone that can sometimes be broken apart by hand, making limestone-rich areas a great place to start fossiling. However, there are many inland sites and I found some great fossils in a sandstone quarry back in the summer near Oxford. River banks can also be good places to search.

You will need a rock hammer which will cost about £10 for a basic model and can be purchased from internet retailers. On my first fossiling expedition many years ago I took a household hammer but this is crude and you can end up smashing up the fossils you are trying to extract which sort of defeats the object (and I got nasty looks from experienced fossilers as I laid into the rock face with my claw hammer).

There are two ways to look at this. Firstly, you can find the fossils and leave them part exposed in their matrix (this is the technical name for the rock that surrounds the fossil). You can then sell these to fossil collectors who advertise on the internet or you can sell them directly on eBay. Raw fossils like this can go from a few pounds up to £50 if you get a really good large specimen.

The second approach is that you can add value to your fossil by patiently chipping it out of the matrix and then polishing it up. This will enable you to sell it for a higher price (again to a dealer or direct). Obviously the second option will take time to learn the techniques and also time to do the work so if you're looking for quick turnaround then go for the former. However, beautifully restored fossils can generate hundreds of pounds and it could open the door to an interesting new hobby and revenue generating exercise. Also this hobby is great fun, young and old alike can't help but feel a real sense of our place in the universe by holding the remains of an animal that lived 200 million years ago.

Useful info: www.ukfossils.co.uk (this site is brilliant and gives you tips on where to find fossils) and the Dorling Kindersley handbook on fossils by David Ward

Tips: check you are allowed to take fossils.

Some areas are protected such as nature reserves. Avoid disused mines (see any episode of Lassie to get firsthand evidence of the outcomes that are likely to ensue if time is spent in or near disused mines). Fossil fairs and exhibitions are a good place to get advice or make contacts (see www.ukfossils.co.uk as above)

Risk	
Return	££
Time	⊕⊕⊕⊕
Training	📖

36
Freecycle trading

From sofas to curtain poles to posters, freecycle is a grassroots worldwide network, where people give away stuff they don't want any more for free, rather than taking it to the municipal tip as landfill waste.

There is a valuable social element to this project in that it is not only ecologically beneficial but it matches up people who don't want 'stuff' with people who want 'stuff'. However, there is a secondary benefit for those out there who are prepared to do a little work. For example, there is nothing to stop you finding an old chest of drawers and doing it up, adding a little bit of your personal flair and then selling it!

If you are a bit skint it's an honourable way to make some money. This idea fits in particularly well if you are developing your eBay or car booting methods of making an extra bit of dosh. If you are technically minded this can also work in your favour. The cost of consumer electrics these days are so low that it is not worth repairing items that stop working and people simply upgrade and chuck out the incumbent bit of gear. If you have a flair for electricals then you could consider reconditioning items that are thrown away and then selling them.

I myself have used freecycle extensively to get rid of stuff and I would ask that you don't simply take from the scheme. As a member of your local group, you should also offer online any items you don't need any more as it keeps the idea going and growing.

The nature of freecycling is that the person who claims the item must come and get it within a certain time (usually the 'Three Day Rule' applies) so it's an excellent way to recycle unwanted goods and at no cost. As you would expect, any items you advertise on this website need to be legal and the list of banned goods include alcohol, firearms, pornography, drugs or tobacco. Also, bizarrely, the main website suggests that you shouldn't list humans (that's what dating agencies are for).

Your local group has probably taken up the 'two strikes and you're out' rule, so act appropriately if you don't want to antagonise local people. The groups are run by volunteers, and chances are a few people in the streets around you are freecycling already. Originally from the USA, the first group over here was set up six years ago and has grown to a staggering 486 groups nationally. So, if you think there is something you can add value to then be prepared to act quickly.

Useful info: www.freecycle.org

Tips: you will need transport to collect items you claim

Risk	💣
Return	£
Time	🕓
Training	**zero**

37
Fruit and veg picking

If you're relatively fit and strong and love the great outdoors, then fruit or veg picking is perfect for you. The general season for picking is June to September, when strawberries, apples and hops are ready for harvest; gooseberries are ready from early June to mid-July, plums and apples in late August, while apples and pears are harvested in September.

You get paid either a daily rate, an hourly rate or a 'piece' rate, in other words, how much you pick. Daily rates vary but start from around £25. Many farms also offer a campsite for you to pitch your tent but may make a small charge for this, too. You don't need any previous experience or qualifications, just enthusiasm and an ability to work very hard. Once you've been shown how to pick the fruit or veg properly, you'll find you speed up very quickly.

Obviously you're at the mercy of the weather and if it rains heavily, you will have to stop work and this stoppage isn't paid for. There are fruit and veg picking opportunities in Europe, from apple picking in France to strawberry picking in Denmark, so you could have a cheap holiday, too. You'll need plenty of old clothes, suncream and insect repellant and a good head for heights if you're up a ladder every day.

Fruit pickers say that the social scene is what keeps them going – it's a great way to meet new people. Alternatively, if you just want to cut food costs and stock up on fruit for your freezer, then consider the pick-your-own route. Many farms offer this and it can also be a great family day out – kids love picking fruit.

Basic farm etiquette needs to be observed like walking carefully down the rows, not eating too much as you pick, being aware of the dangers of farm machinery and closing gates behind you.

Useful info: look in the local press for farm adverts or go to www.pickyourown.org for a list of farms in your area. For seasonal work, go to www.pickingjobs.com, www.anyworkanywhere.com and www.moneymagpie.com

Tips: ask around at farmers' markets and rural pubs for work

Risk	
Return	££
Time	☺ ☺ ☺
Training	zero

38
Gambling

You can't really have a guide to making money without mentioning gambling. From spread betting to the lottery to poker to bingo the appeal of winning big without having to do anything other than punt out a bit of your money seems like an almost universal human failing.

Having been an avid studier of the wealthy it seems that the most sure-fire route to riches is hard work and a modicum of luck. We all know the statistical improbability of winning the lottery yet each week millions of people continue to do it. For those of you tempted to gamble to make extra money I would most certainly advise you against it because, quite simply, you will not.

If you must gamble look on it as entertainment and your stake is the cost of that entertainment. If you end up with more than your stake you've been lucky. If you lose your stake you've enjoyed the experience. If you can't afford to lose the stake don't do it. It's the last refuge of the desperate. A mug's game.

Risk	💣💣💣💣💣
Return	£
Time	☺ ☺ ☺
Training	📖

39
Gift cards

Time-consuming but lucrative, making gift cards is a great way to put your artistic talents to use. It goes without saying that practise makes perfect and your first attempts may resemble the work of a young child, but there are many different craft websites which supply a whole range of glittery and shiny bits and bobs to add panache to your creations. The more professional and original they look the better and with the card market as competitive as it is, finding your own style is ideal.

Many different occasions warrant all sorts of cards, from birthdays, to anniversaries to congratulations, so there are no end of opportunities. You will need good quality materials to make the best cards and there are many websites devoted to craft and card making.

Expect to sell your cards for less than the shops, around £1.50 per card, while a pack of craft materials to make 100 cards will set you back around £25.

If you're not hugely confident, then consider a short course to brush up on your design skills. Ask at your local community centre, check local press or look online. Give your cards as much exposure as possible and display them at craft fairs, car boot sales and even sell them online. There are websites that will host your collection, but will take a 10% bite out of your profits, so shop around for the best deal, check out www.fotopic.net for more information.

Useful info: for craft materials, try www.artymiss.co.uk and www.essentialcraftbits.co.uk or even the online internet craft fair www.craft-fair.co.uk

Tips: get the whole family involved and speed up production

Risk	💣✴
Return	££
Time	🕐🕐🕐
Training	📖

40
Grant grabbing

Although it's not really in the spirit of this book to encourage people to sit back and get money for not actually doing anything it has to be pointed out that as a tax payer (assuming you have done some work in your life) you are entitled to all sorts of money from the government in the form of grants. Talk to your local council and see what is available as many grants each year remained unclaimed because people simply don't know they are available. The main areas where these grants are available are as follows:

Environmental

The government is trying to encourage us to reduce our impact on the environment. Installing energy-saving heating and insulation will make your house warmer and save you money; an average saving of up to £200 per year can be made.

The Government, energy suppliers and local authorities all provide grants to help you implement energy saving measures. The best place to start is the Government's Energy Saving Trust (EST), www.energysavingtrust.org.uk. Although this is not technically a way to make money, if you were thinking of having loft insulation anyway then why not apply for a grant and get some cash towards it.

Home improvement

You might not know that if you are elderly or on a low income your local Home Improvement Agency (HIA) can help to repair, improve or maintain your home. There are around 300 not for profit, locally based HIAs around the country that can help in varying ways. Check with your local council for HIAs in your area.

For the disabled

A Disabled Facilities Grant is available from your local council to help towards the cost of adapting your home if you, or someone living in your property, is disabled. The grant is for work that is essential to help a disabled person live an independent life. Contact the council's housing or environmental health department for further information.

Utility arrears

As well as grants to make your home more energy efficient some utility companies also offer them to help if you have arrears on your gas, electricity or water bills. Schemes are offered for gas and electric by British Gas Energy Trust, EDF Energy Trust, Npower First Step. Water schemes are run by Anglian Water Trust Fund, Bristol Water, Dwr Cymru/Welsh Water, Severn Trent Trust Fund, Southern Water, Thames Water Customer Assistance Fund, Three Valleys Water, Wessex Water, Yorkshire Water Community Trust.

Local council grants

There may also be other grants for your home available from your local council. As councils can offer different funding, search for details on your council's website or contact them to ask for more information.

Useful info: visit the brilliant website run by Martin Lewis, www.moneysavingexpert.com

Tips: don't feel guilty – if you've worked and paid your dues then you deserve these.

41
Handy man / man with van

If you love DIY and are confident about tackling most jobs around the home, then setting yourself up as a handy man is ideal. It's the small jobs that you'll be asked to do, the ones no-one else wants or knows how to do.

In essence, you'll need to be a jack of all trades and your jobs could range from changing taps, fixing leaks, hanging doors, repairing showers, replacing locks, bleeding radiators to assembling furniture.

You'll need insurance and references, as well as the tools of your trade, some of which you could hire if necessary. Customers will expect a guarantee for your work, and the usual is twelve months. Set yourself high standards of workmanship – what's acceptable in your own home may fall short in a customer's eyes, and remember to keep your working area extremely clean and tidy.

Rates vary but most handyman will charge anywhere between £30–£50 per job, depending on the nature of the job and the labour involved, so if you build up a broad customer base and are quick and efficient, you should find the work lucrative. As ever, word of mouth recommendation is the key to building up business, but flyers and a board outside your customer's home should boost bookings.

If you have a van and can set yourself up as 'man with a van', consider light removals, deliveries and collections. The drawbacks are that addresses can be difficult to find, not to mention red or yellow lines that customers have neglected to tell you about, as well as awkward items that are heavy or bulky. Before accepting work, check carefully what you will be moving in your van, as you want to avoid building and household waste because you have to pay to dispose of this rather than dropping it at the household tip.

On average, you could charge around £30 per hour. If you don't own a van, consider a contract rental for a short term period; for example, a small van can costs from around £150 a month.

Useful info: for tips and advice go to www.ultimatehandyman.co.uk and www. handymanplus.co.uk. There is also www. vanman.co.uk for ideas

Tips: book a handyman to do a small job in your own home and watch them as they work for ideas and inspiration

Risk	
Return	££
Time	⏰⏰⏰
Training	📖

42
Home shopper

For the men out there the idea of being a professional shopper might be hell on earth. I would rather have a candle-lit dinner with Dean Gaffney than go to Ikea. So at risk of sexual strereotyping I think this one is probably for the girls.

If you love shopping and trawling the high street stores for bargains and pouring over websites for the best deals then put these

shopping skills to best use and set up a home shopper service. Some people are unable to go shopping or just far too busy and need someone with your savvy to get their groceries in double quick time with savings to boot.

Efficient, affordable and reliable should be your mantra, along with charging a competitive hourly rate, around £5. For groceries, you could order them all online for your customers and have them delivered direct to their home – they might not be computer literate so you are providing a service and you are free of any storage or delivery hassles.

The four big online supermarkets are Tesco, Asda, Sainsbury's and Ocado, so depending on your customers' tastes, you can shop at each, collecting valuable Nectar points at Sainsbury's and Club Card points at Tesco along the way. You could also hunt down the best deals between the four by visiting www.mysupermarket.co.uk.

For non-grocery shopping, be it clothes, gifts or items for the home, then charge accordingly for your time spent searching in shops and return trips to take

unsuitable items back. Don't forget that for toiletries, perfume and toys, you can collect Advantage points at Boots, which is also online at www.boots.com.

The drawback is you may have to pay upfront, and, if the customer isn't completely happy with what you've purchased on their behalf, it may take time to receive your fee. Remember to charge for parking and petrol costs.

If your customers are housebound, the likelihood is that they will be unable to unpack a big grocery shop, so a follow-up service could be included whereby you unpack for them and tidy their cupboards and fridge as you go.

A small advert in your local paper could be a good way to promote your service and you should also consider putting leaflets through people's doors. A more targeted campaign would be to offer your services to retirement flats and apartments as this age group are independent but might need some assistance if their health prevents them from driving. Often retirement villages will have a warden or central office who could put up a notice in the common areas or arrange to post flyers in doors.

Tips: practise how fast you can order a weekly shop online and memorise the layout of your local department stores and the bargain bins

Risk	
Return	£
Time	⏰ ⏰
Training	📖

43

Home tutoring

When you think of home tutoring you probably think of little Jonny getting a few hours a week after school to help him pass his math's exams. But it's not just children who want home tutoring; for a spell a few years ago I used to have someone come to our house to teach me guitar lessons (I was rubbish, all thumbs, so I stopped). And it's not just music, if you live a busy life you can have home tutoring for just about everything from Polish to pole dancing, from photography to poker. And if you happen to be skilled in Polish, pole dancing, photography or poker then you can turn it into a money-making exercise.

For children's education a recession will increase the demand for home tutors as the hard up middle classes opt for coaching over prohibitively expensive private schooling. If you can teach a school subject you can expect to earn about £25 an hour. Non-academic subjects will not earn you as much but can still be lucrative. A set of 6 x 3 hour guitar lessons can be charged at £100.

You can advertise your services locally and, particularly with children's education, if you are good word of mouth will spread quickly to the extent that you are likely to have to turn away

work. More general pastimes can be advertised in your local paper or in specialist shops and centres. For example, your local music shop will probably let you stick up a card if you wanted to teach an instrument. Think where your local client base will visit and try and promote your services there.

Useful info: Personal Tutors (www.personal-tutors.co.uk), First Tutors (www.firsttutors.co.uk), the UK's largest database of private tutors, or www.localtutor.co.uk all specialise in matching students with tutors covering school subjects. Tutors with more general skills should log onto www.setyourrate.com. List your skill and set your asking rate and it will match you with prospective clients

Risk	
Return	££
Time	⏰ ⏰ ⏰
Training	📖 📖

44
House clearance

This is not open to everyone as you'll need a bit of time on your hands and also a van. You'll also be lifting stuff so will need some muscles. Venturing into house clearance will mean you have to be prepared for anything – from bereaved relatives to abandoned homes to those that are overrun with vermin.

It's not a job you can do alone, and most customers will expect you to turn up with a few helpers as well as a couple of trucks to take away the rubbish – aim to clear a three-bedroom house in three hours.

You will need to obtain a licence to carry

waste from the environment agency and have a valid permit to use your local municipal tip. Most house clearance companies will recycle wherever possible and have strong environmental ethics, so when promoting your services flag up your green credentials, too. You could also take any bedding, curtains or clothing to charity organisations. Ensure you know how to disconnect big kitchen appliances, like washing machines, fridges and ovens and invest in the right tools. You might be able to sell some of the items on eBay (see page 40).

You may also be asked to clear garages, sheds and lofts, so be prepared for some heavy duty, dirty work. Most customers will prefer not to be there when you clear a house, often because it's a house of a recently deceased relative, so remain sensitive to this and if you come across items of value, like antiques, you could offer to sell them for the customer, if necessary, and reduce the fee accordingly.

Rates for house clearance are negotiable, depending on the location and size of the house and, of course, how much stuff there is to clear, but on average taking away a truck full of junk costs from £250. Van hire will be your main outlay, so research local van hire companies for the best deals, expect to pay around £50 for a couple of days, but a better deal might be had on a weekly or monthly basis.

Contact your local council to see if you can get on their approved list for domestic clearance. Also consider offices and shops. The recession is causing businesses to close at an alarming rate and commercial landlords are often left with premises full of equipment because when firms go bust most employees are not worried about cleaning up after they have lost their jobs.

Useful info: for van hire go to www.thrifty. co.uk

Tips: invest in protective clothing and face masks and practise disconnecting the washing machine. Remember to lift with your legs keeping your back straight. Invest in a trolley

Risk	🌑🌑
Return	££
Time	🕐🕐🕐
Training	📖

45
House sitting

The crime rate has dropped year on year since 1995 but this is not expected to always be the case. Police have recently announced that they anticipate an increase in acquisitive crime as the recession bites deeper. Yes, this means that as you pick up this book to think of ways of making an extra bit of dough other less scrupulous people will be supplementing their income by nicking stuff. So when people have to leave home for a while, their main worry will be the security of their property.

This is where a house sitter is invaluable and if you would enjoy living in someone else's home then this is a great job to try. The plus side is that it is for short-term periods, from a week to a month, and the homeowner will often leave you a fridge and freezer full of food as an incentive to get good people (although this is not always the case so make sure you check your entitlements before embarking on the job).

Your responsibilities will often include looking after pets and general maintenance such as watering the plants and mowing the lawn. The homeowners will spend their time away happy and confident that that burglars and vandals are not residing in their lovely mock Tudor mansion using their state of the art kitchen to cook microwave burgers and with the added bonus that Fifi, the pedigree hamster, is getting fresh carrots every morning.

Most people will approach an agency to supply their house sitter, although it's also worth advertising your services in the classified ads if they are cheap enough. Also consider posting flyers with your credentials. Agencies tend to employ house sitters who are retired professionals with great references, with rigorous police checks, so bear this in mind (retired colonels are always in demand as they are by nature respectful but are more than capable of using their twelve bore on any would be scallywags).

If you do take up a house sitting job, be prepared for everything from calling in plumbers to fix burst pipes to escorting poorly pets to the vets to taking phone messages for the homeowners. The downside is that your idea of home comfort might be quite different from the home owners, so you may have to make allowances in terms of how many hot baths you can have and the type of food in the fridge, plus you'll have to keep the place clean. In general the big-name agencies charge around £30 per day, on top of which is a charge for pet care.

Useful info: www.homesitters.co.uk and www.g-angels.co.uk for more information

Tips: take all your favourite treats, it's like a holiday after all, but remember the drinks cabinet is a no-no

Risk	
Return	££
Time	☺ ☺ ☺
Training	zero

46
Internet surveys

Like focus groups, paid for internet surveys provide market feedback on a host of products and services. Unlike focus groups you don't have to go and make small talk with a bunch of strangers and you can do it in the luxury of your own home. You get paid to fill out the survey and the company gets some good honest opinions about what consumers think.

Let's be realistic, you are not going to get rich with this one. Companies will pay good money for focus groups because of the physical nature of it they know they have your undivided attention for a few hours. With online surveys they know they don't have your full attention and for this reason the rates are significantly lower.

Also beware of the scammers out there. Sites promising to earn you hundreds of pounds (or often dollars) are not being truthful and are often scam sites where they are trying to get money off you for registering with them. If you are asked for money or your credit card details run a mile.

Yougov is an independent market research company that compiles information for the government and other organisations, particularly media companies. You often see Yougov quoted on the bottom of news items on television or at the bottom of surveys commissioned by newspapers (75% of people think Gordon Brown looks a bit cross). Typically you will get paid 50p per survey and when you reach £50 they will send you a cheque. You will need to be a UK resident and over 18 to participate and, obviously, have a computer and internet access.

Useful info: www.lightspeedpanel.com and www.yougov.com

Tips: be realistic about what you can earn to avoid disappointment. Anyone offering to pay you hundreds of ££ is lying

Risk	💣※
Return	£
Time	🕐🕐
Training	**zero**

47
Knife sharpening

We were going to put hairdresser in here but then we researched it and realised that to actually do this you're going to need a lot of training which doesn't really help you to make money now – by the time you complete your training the recession will probably be over. If you decided to wing it, skip the training and then tout yourself around as a bona fide crimper then you're going to be very unpopular and probably end up getting run out of town. Or lynched. People take their barnets very seriously. You can gamble with my pension all you like, but muck my fringe up and you're dead!

One of the tips of being a hairdresser was buying a good pair of scissors and keeping them sharp. This indirectly led us on to another money-making scheme. In times gone by there were people who came to your house and sharpened your knives. Indeed they were quite common and occupied the same place in society as the rag and bone man or the tinker.

But like so many things in our throwaway culture they dwindled away because the cost of purchasing new knives is very cheap. However, my money-making mavericks, in a recession people keep an eye on the little costs like buying new kitchen knives when their existing ones get blunt. And folk are also going to be eating in more and going out less which means more home cooking.

But couldn't a person with a blunt knife buy a sharpener and do it themselves, I hear you say. Well, yes they could but few sharpeners are really very good and once people experience the swede-splitting joy of a professionally rejuvenated blade they'll be hooked.

You'll need to buy a commercial knife sharpener from your nearest catering supply company. The I.O Shen is acknowledged to be the best in the industry and costs £269 which is expensive but can bring a knife to a razor-edge in a few seconds. Lesser models are available from as low as £100. Expect to be able to charge £1 a knife. On the basis that most people have at least half a dozen chopping knives you could expect to get £5 from a household. If you got ten households in a street on a Saturday morning that's £50!

If you had a van you could do this on the premises which would be preferable from a customer service viewpoint as you could have them back in minutes which makes your service very convenient. Alternatively you could collect and return the next day but strangers might not want you walking off with their Sabatier set.

The best way to market this service is to pick a reasonably prosperous area and knock on doors and advertise yourself. Have some flyers or business cards made up which you can post through the door if people are not in. Set to return to these routes a few months later and you are likely to build up a nice little client base this way.

Useful info: buy some plasters

Tips: practice on your own knives and those of your friends and neighbours before unleashing yourself on the public at large. If you are knocking on doors don't do it too late as people don't like strangers knocking on their doors in the night

Risk	💣
Return	£
Time	🕐
Training	📖

48
Knitting agent

I'm throwing this idea out there for free to see if one of my ideas can be turned into an industry! To my knowledge nobody is currently doing this and if you can get this off the ground then I would really like to know because it would make me proud. Let us know on the website www.101guides.co.uk.

Three facts: three million people currently knit or craft with yarn (crocheting). The population of the UK is about 62 million (although nobody seems to be entirely sure what our population is these days) and, as I write this, the temperature outside is -1°. The third fact is that I hardly ever see anyone wearing hand knitted gear these days.

So with all those people and allowing for our particular brand of British weather there is a need for warm clothing and we are entering a prolonged period of economic downturn. And, to cap it all off, global warming seems to be making it colder (no, I don't understand that either).

Now it is likely that you know someone who knits. Mrs G's grandmother knits. Endlessly. And she churns out the most fantastic articles and my kids love them to bits. And what's more they are unique which means my kids are unlikely to ever encounter the horror of bumping into another child wearing the same sweater on the high street (that's a joke by the way).

Many grandmothers will knit scarves and cardies and polo necks and just give them away because they don't have the commercial acumen to make it pay. A local lady is currently knitting a scarf that is three miles long because she loves knitting but lacks people to give her scarves to and the creative spur to turn her skill in a more lucrative direction. But we're going to change that.

What I propose is a way for you and your granny to make a bit of coin. So what you need to do is this. There are hundreds of knitting websites (www.dailyknitter.com as an example) which provide free patterns. Find one you like that you think is commercially desirable and provide your knitter with the pattern and a supply of wool with which to make it. Ask her if she has any friends that want to do the same thing. If she lives in an old people's home then even better, send round some leaflets. Pop an advert in the local paper. So far you are going to have spent some money on wool and a small bit of local advertising.

The next bit is clever. You sell the knitted products at your next local craft fair and you pay your knitters 25% of the sale price. You could also slot this into your eBay activities. I acknowledge it's a bit risky but let's assume you pay £10 for the wool and you get £50 for the jumper. Even with the 25% commission and the cost of the craft fair or eBay it's still possible to make a nice margin.

Let me know how you get on!

Tips: network within groups of elderly ladies.

Risk	some wool
Return	not known
Time	not known
Training	zero

49
Leaflet and paper distribution

This is not particularly glamorous I know but one sector that is particularly buoyant is the home delivery/fast food sector and they all require leaflets to be put through people's doors. But it's not just pizza parlours; there are hundreds of companies who will pay you to deliver flyers, leaflets, letters, brochures and free sheet newspapers in your local area.

Companies who organise mail drops can usually be found advertising in the job section of local newspapers or community websites. The local employment centre may also advertise or you could even talk to local takeaways to see if they will pay you directly to do certain areas.

As I have said it's not the most glamorous work but it does have some advantages. You will do a lot of walking so it's good for your fitness. There are not many jobs that actually contribute to your physical wellbeing. Most of these delivery jobs are freelance so you can increase this sort of work or stop doing it altogether if other more lucrative cash generating exercises come along. This work also tends to be fairly flexible so you can do it when it suits you be it during the day when your kids are at school or at weekends and evenings if you work during the day or are juggling a few money-making schemes.

Avoid firms who offer you a percentage of the sale rather than a delivery fee. A flat fee per hour or per number of items delivered is the best policy as you can calculate what you are going to earn relative to how much you put in. Expect to earn between £5 and £8 an hour depending on the route, the items delivered and how fast you work.

Tips: wear comfortable shoes. Agree the rates before you start. Insist on weekly payment

Risk	💣
Return	£
Time	🕐 🕑
Training	zero

50
Local councillor

Are you opinionated? Do you have a view on everything? Do you spend a lot of time getting upset about local issues? Are you a long-term resident? Do you like concerning yourself with other people's affairs? Do you like to rant but nobody listens? If the answer to these questions is yes then you might be suited to local politics.

Instead of complaining about things, get your sleeves rolled up and get involved. Make a difference. And here's the clincher, you get paid! OK, it's not pay in the way you might expect, not like a real salary. It's called the members allowance scheme and it provides elected members with a contribution towards the cost of being a councillor. Being a councillor is not supposed to be a full-time job, but you are elected to represent your ward and the interests of the people who live there.

A note of caution, this is hard work and effective councillors can work up to 20 hours per week so although it is not full time it can take up a lot of your time and will require real commitment. In the past the role of councillor was unpaid but because the responsibility and work load has mounted up over the years the allowance scheme was introduced.

Every four years the council will hold elections and if you want a seat then you must stand for election. This will mean you have to get yourself known in your local ward and tell people what you stand for. If you win the seat then you will be accountable to the people who voted you in so don't take this lightly. If you think it's an easy few quid for not doing anything then you are wrong. The amount of money paid varies between councils but expect to get an annual allowance of between four and six thousand pounds per year plus you will also get expenses towards computing equipment, stationery postage, travel and parking.

To become a councillor there are some requirements: you must be at least 18 years of age on the day you are nominated and you must be a British citizen. You will also need to have lived or worked in your local area for the past 12 months. If you have recently been made bankrupt or have come out of prison you will have to wait a few years to be considered.

Useful info: call your local council or visit their website. For further information visit www. communities.gov.uk

Tips: if you think politics is boring then probably not for you. If you want to make a difference to people's lives then go for it

Risk	●
Return	££
Time	⊕ ⊕ ⊕ ⊕ ⊕
Training	📖 📖 📖

51
Make chutney and jam

Home-made chutney and jam are a great way to use up seasonal fruit and vegetables like plums, rhubarb, tomatoes and apples, as well as saving you money. They make lovely gifts and sell well at markets and fêtes. Chutney has a sweet and sour taste due to the balance of sugar and vinegar while jam is a perennial favourite, whether smooth or fruity and chunky.

You'll need the right equipment to achieve the best results, so along with the usual kitchen equipment like scales and chopping boards, invest in a stainless steel preserving pan, a sugar thermometer for the jam, jars, waxed lids with a cellophane cover, elastic bands, heatproof jugs, long-handled spoons, sieves and labels.

Chutney recipes involve mixing the chopped fruit or vegetables with spices, sugar and vinegar, and then slow cooking until it's a smooth pulp. For jam, the fruit is cooked and brought to simmer at a certain temperature. It then needs to be tested for a 'setting' consistency, so follow recipes to the letter if you want to achieve the right consistency.

The downside is that if you're inexperienced in the kitchen, it'll take a fair bit of practise to get the recipes right, so be prepared for a few failed batches and wasted fruit. If the waxed discs and cellophane are not the right size, air will get into the jam and chutney and turn them mouldy – disastrous if you intend to make big batches to sell. You'll need to ensure that the jars you use are all sterilised by plunging them into boiling water for ten minutes, before drying them in the oven, upside down, at gas mark 3/160C/325F. One friend sterilizes her jars by using her old baby bottle sterilizer that she still had hanging around.

Chutney should have a deep, earthy flavour and needs at least three months to mature – no cutting corners or rushing.

Organic jams and chutneys sell online for around £3.50 a jar, while in the supermarkets they sell at around £1.50, so price accordingly.

If you can afford to splurge, an online jam making kit can cost around £75, see www.bakersandlarners.co.uk. For equipment, all good supermarkets should have what you need or alternatively go to an online retailer like www.lakeland.co.uk.

You can sell your jam directly to the public at farmers' markets and fêtes but this can be expensive and knock out a lot of your profit. Become a wholesaler and sell locally to a deli or someone who has a stand at one of the farmers' markets.

Useful info: go to www.bbcgoodfood.com or www.jam-recipes.co.uk for recipes. Also check out www.allotment.org.uk, www.storingandfreezing.co.uk and www.makingyourown.co.uk

Tips: somewhere along the line you will burn yourself with hot liquid, so make sure you have the first aid kit ready

Risk	
Return	£
Time	⊙ ⊙ ⊙
Training	📖

52
Masseuse

No naked bodies, no scented oil and no funny business. Pure and simple head and shoulder massage is perfect if you would like to train as a therapist but don't want to get too close, plus it's one that needs no previous experience. It's renowned to be a great holistic therapy that gives good results, easing stress and eliminating tense knots in the shoulders.

You can attend one-day diploma courses or evening classes but remember you will need professional indemnity insurance. If you have head massage experience, then don't miss out on the latest trend that's taking off in bars, clubs and at corporate events – an Urban Chill head massage. Get in on the action and train as a 'chiller', someone who administers a speedy 5–15 minute massage and is paid on what the client feels it's worth from £2.50 to £40 (so make it good and deep). You have to be committed to the cause, however, to secure your place on a training course, and Urban Chill asks you to send in your CV and a photo, along with details as to how you're the ideal candidate. If selected, you face the interview process and have to pass an assessment, then you're on to a £25 training course (plus £25 for the uniform).

The plus side is that you get to have a great night out while working and meet new people and gain valuable experience. Drawbacks include drunk clients who refuse to pay, stressed clients who argue about how much to pay and amorous clients who want to pay in another way. Whatever, crack your knuckles and go for it.

For details go to www.urban-chill.com or check out local courses online or in the local press. There's a wealth of choice, and some companies are more unscrupulous than others, charging exorbitant fees and promising accreditation with institutes and consortiums, so step carefully.

Tips: practise on friends and family to get that 'oooh' effect

Risk	💣
Return	££
Time	⊙ ⊙ ⊙
Training	📖 📖

53
Mobile disco

"Oooh, oooh, oooh, oooh stayin' alive..." If you know your music and can work your way around some turntables, you could give this a shot. All you need is good, reliable equipment, a stack of floor fillers and a crowd-pleasing manner.

Suffice to say that buying brand new equipment is going to break the bank, so look for second hand bargains online or in the small ads. An alternative is to hire the equipment, which can cost from £150 for a weekend, depending on your requirements (for ideas go to www.diydiscohire.co.uk). You need confidence and a knack off dealing with electricals (the equipment can be complicated) and you should ensure that all the equipment you work with is safe and carries a Portable Appliance Testing certificate. You'll need public liability insurance to protect

yourself and partygoers if anything goes wrong.

It's not just about the sounds though, your client will want an awesome light show, so check out YouTube for how to do it. Most clients will want guarantees that, if due to circumstances beyond your control, you fail to show up, someone else will, so have contingency plans in place. This will be featured in your contract with the client, as well as details about how they should pay you and the deposit you require.

The average price for a DJ at a disco is around £300, and if you charge much less than this people may start asking why. You could specialise in one area, the 1980s for example, and then there will be no doubt as to the type of tunes you will be playing. You need to be open-minded and accept your clients will have a playlist, but perhaps in the contract limit the playlist to 10 songs, so you're not at the mercy of someone who doesn't have a clue.

Useful info: if you're keen but lacking in skills, think about a DJ course, www.musiceverything. com, for example, to learn the trade and to pick up valuable industry tips and advice

Tips: unless you're at a Seventies-themed party, resist calling out for everyone to 'boogie on down'. Set up in the front room and practise mixing on the decks

Risk	
Return	££
Time	🕐 🕐 🕐
Training	📖 📖

54
Mobile phone selling

Most mobile phone companies will let you upgrade your phone each year and my wife and I like to take advantage of this (actually I do, she just wants something with big buttons on). As a consequence my desk drawer has lots of perfectly workable phones in it that I don't have the heart to throw away because it seems wasteful.

But then all that changed – one of the book researchers told us about a type of website that purchases your used phones. Both www. money4urmobile.com and www.mazumamobile. com will pay you cash for your phone. You simply type in the model of phone and the serial number, they then send you a prepaid envelope into which you pop your phone and then post it. They then send you the payment for the phone. Incredibly what I thought was worthless rubbish is actually worth £30.

Most of the phones are used in emerging markets such as China, India and Africa. So you're earning some money and you're saving the planet. Excellent! Also while you are scouring your carboot sales to keep an eye open for mobiles that people assume are completely without value but can be recycled and turned into wonga.

There is another sell your phone opportunity. When your contract has expired and it's time to upgrade and sign again it can be an exciting time. You wait in anticipation for the courier to come. You pop out to get some milk and in the few seconds you are out they attempt their delivery and drop one of those annoying postcards through the door to say that they tried to deliver but you weren't in (for, like, four minutes!) and that your beautiful state of the art phone with 10 mega pixels and 500 ring tones and a little thing that goes ping is currently sitting in a warehouse in Coventry 30 miles away awaiting your collection. But you don't have time to get it until the weekend so you get even more excited, the distance between you and your new gadget making your heart grow even fonder as you imagine its sleek lines nestled comfortably in your pocket, 'Ride of the Valkyries' programmed on the ring tone with the vibrate set to react in tandem. Once you've got your phone you will be truly happy. Complete. And then Saturday comes and you and the wife and kids all pile in the car and head over to an industrial estate in Coventry, all the time the excitement rising, where you join a queue of apprehensive males all wringing their hands, not talking, waiting, waiting for their new handsets. And then and then…. This is where you do something you have never done before. You take off the courier company plastic bag and instead of impatiently tearing open the box (and wondering why they need to pack so much stuff round it) you carefully put it in the boot of the car. What? I hear you say. It's hard I know. But you put it in the boot and you take it home. And you put it on eBay. And you get £150 for it and you continue to use your perfectly good phone which has served you loyally for the past 12 months and will probably last for at least another three years.

The only problem I have with this scheme is that you are paying for the phone through the line rental so all you're really doing is effectively getting money for something that you're going to have to pay back. It's a bit like a bad loan. But it will net you some cash now. I never said this book was going to be clever. If we were writing a book about saving money I would suggest you get an airtime-only contract which will be cheaper.

Tip: search your drawers for your old phones. Ask your friends and family if they have any phones because you want to recycle them (you don't have to tell them about the cash)

Risk

Return	£
Time	⏲
Training	zero

55
Musician

Whether you've plucked at strings, tickled the ivories or tapped out a beat, you shouldn't ignore your musical talent and the cash it could bring you. Look at Paul McCartney, for someone who can't even read music he's done OK for himself. Or that guitar player who was in Blur who spent his whole time drunk and drugged out of his

mind and now spends all his time telling us how drunk and drugged out of his mind he was. OK, let's be honest you're unlikely to be a rock star but there is a few quid that can be made if you have the desire and skill.

Audition for gigs at local pubs and clubs and go along to jam sessions (advertised in local papers and also on www.gumtree.com) to get your name known. The going rate for performing in a restaurant or pub is around £60 for a couple of hours, while a bigger corporate event will be £100 an hour and a wedding would rake in £200 an hour.

Consider going to a recording studio to record a CD of your music, which will cost around £400, plus about £600 to make 1,000 copies, which you could then sell for £10 each. If the thought of street busking appeals, then first check with your local council if there are any regulations. You may earn pennies rather than pounds, but you could sell your CD at the same time (you'll need a street licence). In some cases, authentic buskers are paid to perform at events, so check out www.musicalbusker.co.uk for details (see Busking on page 20).

To achieve maximum exposure, go to a hosting website like www.cdbaby.com where you have your own web page. You can sell your CDs or have your music available for downloads. The company takes 9% of your profits from downloads and $4 from every CD sale.

If performing isn't bringing in enough money, you could teach. Rates for music teachers vary, but for a classical guitar teacher, for example, you can expect to earn up to £30 an hour. You'll need references and, if teaching children, the obligatory police checks. To teach in schools you'll need a knowledge of grades and a great deal of patience.

Tips: practise makes perfect and you might need to join a band, rather than go solo, so check

out live music pubs and clubs for adverts for band members

Risk	🎆🎆
Return	££
Time	🕑🕑🕑
Training	📖📖📖📖

56
Nail technician

Creating stunning false nails is a booming part of the beauty industry (with over 2000 qualified practitioners nationally), so if you want to be a successful nail technician, you'll need training.

To reach salon standards, you should ideally aim for NVQ Level 3 in Nail Services and training courses are available at colleges but if

Name: Joanne Ewins
Full Time job: Sales Manager
Age: 26

Joanne combines a successful role as a Sales Manager of a thriving media firm with an interesting money-making hobby that she just can't leave behind.

I love doing nails. I started with a full-time course in beauty therapy in my late teens and then I became a full-time beauty technician in a local salon.

I really enjoyed doing pedicures and took a one-week intensive course at a college in Windsor (Carlton Institute of Beauty Therapy) and followed this up with night classes which took one night per week. This lead to me becoming an advanced nail technician.

I then worked in various salons in my local area but decided to leave the beauty therapy industry because I wanted to earn more money. Since then I have pursued a career in media sales but I have continued to operate as a freelance nail technician (I now rank top for Warwickshire and Worcestershire).

It's a great business and very sociable. Many of my clients have become friends and I would recommend it as a part-time job if you are good with people. Go along to your local college and see what courses they do. I would recommend a three month introductory course to manicure and pedicure which are usually available either at the college or at a local beauty therapy school. You'll look to be spending only a few hundred pounds to get on this course.

I genuinely have a good time and we often throw manicure parties and have a glass or two of wine and really make it fun. You can charge £18 for a manicure. And once a client finds a good nail technician they NEVER let them go.

Case Study £

you want to develop it as a part-time business or extended hobby there are also private training courses to get you up and running and many charge from around £500 for a four to six day course. They cover the basics of acrylic nail application, as well as health and safety guidelines and the latest trends. It's also worth joining a professional body like the Association of Nail Technicians, www.ant.uk.net, from £45, with tips, advice and how-to videos.

The advantage of this kind of job is that you work around existing commitments such as full-time jobs or children and once you've built up a client base word of mouth is likely to create an increased demand (particularly if you are good). Don't forget to look into your insurance options and you'll need to stock up on equipment, products and a uniform, so check out www.thenailwarehouse.biz and www.nailtechs.co.uk for ideas.

Nail technicians can earn around £11,000 a year and there are a number of job opportunities in beauty salons, health clubs, spas and hairdressers, while the going rate for a false set of nails is around £40.

A set of nails requires ongoing maintenance and you'll find that you quickly build up a customer base as people need repeat treatments. You'll have to have good customer skills and an easy rapport with people, as well as a methodical approach to your work, a good eye for design and nail colour and a steady hand. Like hairdressers you'll be expected to listen to the trials and tribulations of your customers.

Tips: get to work practising on friends and family and ask them to spread the word

Risk	
Return	££
Time	🕐 🕐
Training	📖📖📖

57
Nude modelling

If you think you have a beautiful body, incredible bone structure and you're well proportioned, taking your clothes off to earn money may not seem such a bad idea. The idea of nude modelling is often met with derision and smutty remarks, but in fact you could be helping to create breathtaking art and will be in good company – celebrities who have modelled nude include Kate Moss (while pregnant), Cherie Blair, Sean Connery and Quentin Crisp.

Nude models who pose for artists and sculptors are known as life models and it's not just simply about taking your kit off. It's physically demanding and requires a great deal of patience and commitment. Holding poses for for up to 45 minutes is strenuous and often tutors in art classes will put you in a pose. As you gain experience, you will learn what is comfortable and what's not and may often decide your own poses.

Sometimes, two life models are booked and you may find that you are posing with a member of the opposite sex, so be aware of each other's comfort zones. Life models usually undress behind a screen rather than in front of students and they wear a robe while not posing. As for props, this can vary, from having a chair or steps, to working with ropes, poles and drapes.

Many life models are listed on the Register of Artists' Models, www.modelreg.co.uk, which sets professional standards. It costs £30 a year for membership, but you have to audition. Experienced life models can earn around £10 an hour.

The downside is that you may find that you're not quite as confident as you first thought when it comes to taking off the robe, not to mention problems like cramp, twitches and itches.

You may also find you have to strike the same uncomfortable pose week after week as students learn how to capture it properly. Contact your local university or colleges to see if they have any vacancies.

Tips: if you have a jealous partner make sure you don't tell them where you go on a Monday night!

Risk	💣
Return	£
Time	🕐🕐
Training	📖

58
Party catering

If you've started your sandwich business (see page 89) then a logical progression may well be to supply corporate and social functions. An extension into sandwich platters for board meetings and corporate days out is not a far stretch from what you've already been doing. Offer your service to existing clients who are already happy recipients of your star catering.

Once confident you can start to promote yourself locally for party catering. If you can handle this then the ultimate step is wedding catering. You have to be organised to do this well but if you can develop this side of your business it can be very lucrative and you can expect to charge hundreds of pounds for big celebrations and events.

Tips: try making those little Yorkshire puddings with a tiny slice of beef and a dollop of horseradish. If you can do that then you're onto something

Risk	💣※
Return	£££
Time	✳✳✳✳
Training	📖📖

59
Party plan

Setting up a party plan business doesn't require a big initial investment; you can choose products that you love and you can have fun doing it. It's known as direct selling, whereby you can hold parties either at your own or at other people's houses to sell your goods or you use a catalogue and act as a company's representative. It's usually a case of how much you earn depends on the hours you are prepared to put in.

Some companies offer party plan packs to buy up front, some of which can cost from around £100, and you then decide how much to sell the goods for and ultimately how much profit you make, for example go to www.

usbornebooksathome.co.uk or www.virgin cosmetics.com.

The Direct Selling Association suggests that there are over 30,000 people selling direct on a full-time basis. It lists its member companies online, which adhere to a code of practice and it offers sound business advice: go to www.dsa.org.uk.

The biggest name in the industry has to be Avon with a staggering five million representatives worldwide and you can earn £1 for every £4 you sell, plus it costs only £15 to get started. Alternatively, you could host parties in your home for a cheap night in with friends and receive discounts on the products sold; look, for example, at www.pamperedchef.com.

Advertise in the local press, tap all your friends and your friends' friends for party hosting opportunities and distribute flyers advertising your party. Your main worry is that no-one will want to buy your products, so accept that you can't win them all and regard these as promotional events. Needless to say, price your products fairly and target your audience carefully. Your sales technique will improve over

time and you'll learn when to ease off on the hard sell.

Tips: don't buy an enormous amount of stock for an exorbitant price: a catalogue with samples is the best way to go

Risk	
Return	£££
Time	⏲ ⏲ ⏲ ⏲
Training	📖

60
Pet sitting

If you have a natural affinity with animals, pet sitting is a great opportunity to earn extra cash, especially as it will fit around other commitments you have. Generally, people want pet sitters to come into their home and feed their pets, groom them and give them some companionship while they are away. Often nervous or elderly pets will be much happier at home than moved to a pet boarding facility and it is cheaper for the owners.

For a cat each visit need only be for 20 minutes at either end of the day – dogs will obviously require walking and so allow 40 minutes per visit. You'll need to check out your public indemnity insurance in case you cause damage in the home and it might be worth registering with a pet sitting company for regular bookings, like www.g-angels.co.uk or www.petpals.com. You may need to administer medication, so ask for thorough details on this before the owner goes away.

Ensure there is a contract in place to which you and the owner can refer, listing emergency contact details for security purposes and the vet. You'll be expected to have references and police checks. If you have several pets to visit in a day, then be aware of hygiene and the risk of spreading diseases from one pet to another.

As you are visiting the pets' homes, you'll also be expected to switch on and off lights, check on security and move the post. The average hourly rate for a pet sitter is around £5 per visit, but you could charge more if there are a number of pets to care for and how long it takes to feed and groom them – all negotiable with the owner. It's also worth visiting www.dogsit.com, which is the National Association of Registered Petsitters for useful information.

As with many of these personal services word of mouth is often the most effective marketing but to get it off the ground you could consider popping notes through the doors in your area or alternatively try putting a sign up at your local vets and telling the receptionist about your service.

Tips: don't worry if you can't find the cat – it'll turn up when it's hungry. And some exotic pets look dead but are usually just sleeping

Risk	
Return	£
Time	⏲ ⏲
Training	zero

61
Phone sex operative

One for the ladies here because there does not seem to be many women prepared to pay men to talk dirty to them (perhaps it's because men will probably do it for free). Let's not overanalyse this!

The urban myth of the housewife ironing while she delivers phone sex suggests that this has got to be a money-spinner. If you can fit the calls around your other daily commitments then all well and good.

You'll obviously need a certain knowledge of what a man (or a woman) wants to hear and a strict time limit. You can set up your phone sex line easily but be aware it is a competitive market so you'll need to be imaginative with creating your persona and finding your niche market.

Go to www.adultwork.com and www.fone-me.com for ways to list your service, caller payments and ways to boost business. It's free to register and you can determine whether customers call you or you call them. Needless to say, phone sex is big business and often phone lines charge around £1 per minute, while phone sex operatives earn upwards of £10 an hour.

To build up your experience and knowledge of the industry, try working for one of the established phone sex lines first before venturing out on your own. The downside is that you will need a spare phone and could be asked to work late at night. What's more, there will probably be days (or nights) when you just don't feel like talking dirty.

Also, if you have a busy household, make sure you can tuck yourself away somewhere quiet where you can't be overhead. While not obligatory, you'll be required to fake it and so this might take it out of you.

One way of dipping your toe in this industry is to work for one of the sex text companies like www.text121chat.com which will enable you to try it out at arm's length.

Tips: call a few sample numbers to get into the swing of it and practise on the phone with your partner if they are broadminded

Risk	💣
Return	£££
Time	⏱ ⏱
Training	📖

62
Photographer

Not so long ago this would not have been on this list because to make a living from professional photography was very difficult and certainly not something that people could do on the side to make a bit of extra money. But modern technology and the internet have changed all that.

When you read a newspaper or magazine and you see a picture of an anvil you might assume that we've gone to the trouble of hiring a photographer to go out and photograph an anvil. But your assumption would be wrong because in truth we've purchased the anvil photo from a stock photography company.

A photographer will take the photograph and then supply it to a stock photography company. The stock photography company will then market the picture to media outlets like newspapers, magazines or websites. Once a picture has been sold the photographer will then get a percentage of the price, normally between 20% and 40%. The picture can be sold time and time again and if you have a sharp eye you can often see the same image being used in different mediums.

Then along came istock which enabled people like you and me, rather than just professional photographers, to upload our photographs on to their site and to be paid a royalty percentage on any photographs that istock customers buy.

It has to be said that if you are a rubbish photographer then you're unlikely to get any business but if you have a good eye and a decent camera then you could sell some pictures. Don't send in any of your Aunty Beryl or your cat or your brother's wedding because these are not going to be of interest to web or magazine publishers. But quirky well shot, creative, well lit images that could be used to illustrate a story could sell. You have to

submit your images for approval but if you think you have an eye then this could be a way for you to break into the business.

Another way of making money out of pictures is to become an amateur paparazzo. Big Pictures will buy photos of celebrities from anyone. So, in the unlikely event you see Posh Spice staggering out of a club with her husband (or even better someone other than David Beckham) at two in the morning and you have your camera phone ready, then there is money to be made.

Useful info: check out www.istock.com and www.bigpictures.co.uk

Tips: for istock you will need a good camera and some creative ideas. For Big Picture you just need to be lucky

Risk	
Return	££
Time	✳ ✳
Training	📖 📖

63
Piecework

So-called 'piecework' is when workers are paid per unit that they produce. The history of this form of employment began before the Industrial Revolution, when the automation of jobs such as sewing and the assembly of items was not yet widespread. Payment of this kind is actually a form of performance-related pay; the faster you work, the more money you get.

Nowadays, with machines doing everything, usually faster and better, there is less chance of this type of work. However, there are still some opportunities to be found.

Many homeworkers in the UK are employed in manufacturing, making a wide range of items from footwear to car components. Manufacturers who employ homeworkers don't usually advertise because they will often have a waiting list. They only usually employ people local to their premises so look through your local phone book for manufacturers and ask to be put on a waiting list.

If you are keen on working from home, another possibility is to capitalise on a skill or talent that you have. There is a wealth of information (and indeed work) to be found on the internet. You may consider combining your work with the internet itself; jobs such as home-based technical support are growing in popularity for those who have a good knowledge of computers.

As with any job in which you have no face-to-face contact with your employer, you should always be on the look-out in order to avoid scams.

Useful info: go to www.direct.gov.uk and www.desktoplawyer.co.uk for a full description of your rights, the health and safety consequences of working from home and what the tax implications are

Tips: real jobs don't come with a fee, so never send money up front to people or companies who claim they can give you work at home

Risk	
Return	£
Time	✳ ✳ ✳
Training	📖

64
Porn star

Whether or not you consider porn a legitimate art form there is no doubt that it is big business and it's legal. Although it's not for everyone.

If you think you've got what it takes, then you could earn a great deal. You'll need to get yourself noticed, however, so make a good quality video of yourself in action and have photographs taken that demonstrate your prowess, then upload them to a hosting website, like www.ukmodelsite.com and www.be-seen-here.co.uk and www.starnow.co.uk.

You might want to consider joining a glamour model agency or create your own adult web pages. Websites like www.rollingmodels. com can host them, although it will edit your material where necessary. Try contacting adult entertainment companies direct with your details; www.fullservice.co.uk, for example, employs actors for adult photo and video shoots. If you think you have the confidence, companies like these might ask you to perform in front of a live audience at blue stag nights. You might want to invest in a selection of outfits, so visit www. annsummers.com for inspiration (dominatrix outfits are priced around £40).

If you do decide to go into adult films, then visit www.bgafd.co.uk/miscellany for advice. Most adult movie producers will expect you to carry an up-to-date medical certificate with HIV and STD clearance (and you should check that other performers have a clean bill of health, too).

If you're a man, you need to be at least six inches and you should be able to keep 'excited' for at least two hours, plus you will need to be able to deliver the goods on command. For a boy/girl film, you can expect to earn around £350 per scene, but obviously the more you're asked to do, the more you'll get paid.

Tips: watch adult movies for ideas and inspiration, experiment with your pain and pleasure thresholds and make your own home movies to see how you look

£

Risk	
Return	££
Time	🕐 🕐
Training	📖

65
Private driver

If the idea of working as a private driver appeals, whether as a private taxi or as a chauffeur, expect to earn between £350–£500 per week. You will need a special licence, however, known as a private hire driver's licence, available from your local council and in the London area from the Public Carriage Office; visit www.tfl.gov.uk for more details.

If you aren't in the best of health or have poor eyesight you need not apply because you have to prove a certain level of medical fitness. If you have three years' or more driving experience under your belt, plus a good knowledge of the area that's a good start.The licence requirements are based on those of the DVLA Group 2, details of which can be found at www.dvla.gov.uk.

Many private hire taxi companies ask that you're over 21 and have good spoken English and often that you have a NVQ Level 2 in Road Passenger Vehicle Driving. With companies like these, you sometimes have a car provided that you 'rent' from them and depending on how many account bookings you do, your rental payments decrease. You do get to use the car in your own time, though. You're expected to pay for your own fuel and can accept cash bookings to boost your earnings, as you will be paid a weekly wage for the pre-paid bookings work.

The flexible nature of taxi driving means it can be slotted around existing work commitments and your earnings are directly linked to how

many hours you are prepared to devote to it.

If you want to work for a company or a family as a chauffeur, you will be expected to have all the necessary qualifications, checks, experience and more. You'll often have to wear a uniform, be discreet and sometimes work unsociable hours, but the pay is better than working for a taxi firm. Have a look at the job vacancies on www.masseysagency.co.uk and www.chauffeursearch.co.uk.

Tips: next time you're in a minicab late at night rather than drunkenly ranting to the driver about escalating fuel costs then why don't you chat to him about his job satisfaction

Risk	
Return	££
Time	🕐 🕐 🕐 🕐
Training	📖 📖 📖

66
Promo work

You've seen those motor shows where beautiful girls drape themselves across the bonnet of a Bugatti Veyron and you think 'yeah, I can do that'. And then you wake up. I know that if I draped myself over the bonnet of a Bugatti Veyron (it's a million pound car for those of you who don't watch *Top Gear*) I would probably write it off so let's move away from this example for the time being.

The reality of promotional work is, I'm afraid, not that glamorous. It invariably involves standing around in draughty halls all day getting sore feet while the public at large avoid catching your eye. However for those with a bit of get up and go it can be a rewarding route to make that extra bit of moolah. The most lucrative element of this is promotional work in the sales sector when you can earn a commission on what you sell. But there is an array of non-sales job on offer such as leafleting, draping yourself over things or simply walking around in a bikini or bathing trunks – if you have the physique.

There are thousands of exhibitions each year, from the well known ones such as the Ideal Home Exhibition at London's Earls Court to the lesser known ones such as the Franchise Show in Manchester's Gmex. All of them require staff to man the stands, promote the products and work behind the scenes. Many of these exhibitions and events run over a weekend making them ideal casual work for those with a regular day job.

There are a number of ways you can approach this. You can contact your local exhibition centre and find out about up and coming exhibitions. By visiting the particular exhibition websites you can usually access a list of exhibitors and contact them directly to see if they require your services (try targeting those that are engaged in an activity that you are suited to).

The advantages of this are that you are likely to get a higher pay rate if dealing directly with an exhibitor and you may even strike up a business relationship with them and continue to work for them in the future either at the same venue the following year or at other exhibitions. The disadvantage is that this method of finding work can be time consuming and will not get you work quickly so you might be better off following the second option.

Signing up to an events staffing agency. These companies will sell their services to exhibitors and promotion companies all over the country and will then recruit staff who fit the bill, taking a cut along the way. This saves a lot of time and they can also look after things like tax and NI which is important (as we have said on page 9). Agencies advertise locally or through the larger job websites.

Useful info: www.stuckforstaff.com

Tips: if your employers will allow you, always try to wear comfortable shoes. Most people are not used to being on their feet all day and by mid-afternoon it can hurt. Get commission based schemes agreed in writing before you start work

Risk	
Return	££
Time	⏲ ⏲ ⏲
Training	📖

67
Proofreading

Their are nothin worst than a sentunce with badd grama and speling. It makes the writer look foolish, lazy and badly educated. Which is a bad first impression to leave.

Although computers now provide us with spell check (mine tries to turn everything into American English for some reason and I don't know how to stop it) this is not enough to thoroughly check a book, newspaper, magazine, flyer, brochure or instruction manual before it goes to press or a website before it goes live.

Proofreading involves checking a manuscript or page proof for typing, grammar and spelling errors by the author. Some editors and publishers also ask their proofreaders to spot factual mistakes in the editorial and any potentially libellous statements.

Now if you are an ex-professional footballer with little in the way of education this is not really going to suit you (you should probably open a nightclub in Spain). It is ideally suited to someone with literature and editing experience such as a journalist, editor, teacher or secretary.

The best way to get work is to approach publishers directly. Most of the bigger book and magazine publishers are listed in the *Writers' and Artists' Yearbook* which is available from good bookshops or from Amazon. Also approach newspapers for freelance opportunities. Employment opportunities may also be advertised at the local Job Centre.

Ask each publisher or editor for their house style guidelines to ensure the article has consistency. Most proofreading companies and agents will ask you to complete a proofreading test. You will be expected to meet tight deadlines and if you miss them then you are unlikely to be offered further work.

If you have work experience or professional qualifications in a certain field then try approaching those relevant magazines, journals and papers to offer your services as a proofreader or freelance copy editor.

For those not in the publishing business you can take some home courses which will bring you up to speed. For example, www.train4publishing.co.uk have a distance learning course which costs £385 and can be completed in a few months. With rates of about £10 per hour you should be able to recover the costs fairly quickly.

Useful info: www.train4publishing.co.uk and

Copyediting and Proofreading for Dummies by Suzanne Gilad

Tips: more suited to people with an academic background

Risk	💣
Return	£££
Time	🕐🕐🕐
Training	📖📖📖

68
Psychological research

We've already established that sitting around getting unknown drugs pumped into you can be unpleasant and carries some risk and so may not be suited to everybody. Psychological research is much less invasive than straight medical research.

Like the drug testers you can find work as a psychological research 'guinea-pig' through ads in local papers, student notice boards and on the internet. The experiments are usually quite easy either involving brain scans or simple memory tests. You will be paid cash for your time and your travel expenses. Because the tests are less risky you can expect to get less money.

Useful info: www.biotrax.com

Tips: not for those of a fragile mental state!

Risk	💣
Return	£
Time	🕐
Training	zero

69
Rent a room

If at first the thought of sharing your bathroom with a stranger is offputting, think again. Renting out a room to a lodger could rake in up to £500 a month. What's more the new Rent a Room government scheme entitles you to earn up to £4250 a year (£350 a month), tax free. If you scour websites like www.spareroom.co.uk and www.gumtree.com you can get a fair idea of the rental price of a room in your area.

Before you let anyone move in there are a number of issues to address. First things first, let your insurance company know as this could affect your premium. You also would be well advised to set up a contract, stating rent, when it should be paid, notice periods, house rules, etc. Make an appointment at your local Citizen's Advice Bureau to ensure you have all bases covered. Asking lodgers to set up a standing order avoids any uneasy conversations on the landing about overdue rent.

You'll want to interview possible lodgers, so find out as much as you can about their lifestyle, and expect to spend a lot of time thoroughly checking out their references, organising a credit check www.tenantverify.co.uk, (£15) and even a police check. Don't interview lodgers on your own, ask someone else to be there as you might need another opinion or you may miss something important.

In the first instance, offer the room rental for a short period of time, for example, three months to see how it goes, with the option to extend further if you wish. The ideal room let would be Monday to Friday, so you get the wekends off. Go to www.mondaytofriday.com for information as many people find this a cheaper option than paying to commute or staying in a hotel. Lodgers will expect to use your communal areas and will need a fully furnished room. Usually you would include all the utility bills in the rent (not telephone) and, if you want, you could include meals and cleaning and charge accordingly.

Tips: trust your gut feeling – if there's something you don't like about a potential lodger, even if you can't put your finger on it, be polite and show them the door

Risk	
Return	£££
Time	⏱
Training	zero

70
Rent your car parking space

For easy and hassle-free cash, why not rent out your car parking space, whether it's a driveway, private bay or garage? There are several companies who can list your car parking space on their websites and put you in touch with people who would like to rent them like www.parkatmyhouse.com, www.parklet.co.uk and www.yourparkingspace.co.uk. These companies charge around 10%–15% of your rental fee.

But just how much will you earn? It depends on the location, the more central to town the better. If you live near sport stadiums, shopping centres, airports, train stations or entertainment venues, for example, then your revenue will be greater than if your car parking space is out in the sticks or tucked away on a housing estate.

Most rental websites suggest you could earn around £100 a month, and what's more you can choose to rent out the space on a day-by-day, weekend or weekly basis. If you have a resident's permit bay, then this is the local council's space and not yours to rent out, so forget it.

Let your insurers and your mortgage lender know about the extra use of your property and if you decide to advertise locally under your own steam, seek legal advice and draw up a standard contract to protect your interests. People who want to rent out your garage will want good security, so check locks are working and any windows are secure. If you have a shared driveway to your garage, then alert your neighbours of your plans and ensure that at all times access is clear. Expect to spend some time showing people the space or garage so be honest about the space in adverts and include a picture where possible to avoid any time wasters.

Tips: you'll need to clear out the garage – toys, tumbledriers and bits of old motorbike will put off any prospective customers

Risk	
Return	£
Time	⏱
Training	zero

71
Rent your kids

They sit around all day, eating your food, using your electricity and contributing nothing to the pot. I'm talking about children here. And yet it might be possible to make some money out of the little blighters.

Generally, if they're under 13, you can't get them out earning unless it is in the areas of theatre, television or as a model where the law is slightly different. Your child will need to have a performance licence, which is granted by your local authority, and the local authority will mediate with your child's head teacher to ensure that such activities will not have a direct impact on their education. Your local authority may also insist on a chaperone to keep them up to date on their school work. This usually would only come into force if your child was working on a long-running television series or on a film.

The rules of child modelling/acting:

the golden rule of child modelling seems to be the same as with adult modelling: if an agency demands money from you upfront for 'head shots' or 'acting classes' then you are being scammed. Any reputable agency will take their cut (usually about 20–25%) from the fees the child receives when they have been booked.

Face facts first: Every mum thinks her child is the most beautiful in the world but, as with every type of modelling or acting, it is an extremely competitive industry and you have to be prepared for rejection.

What makes a model child? Some children are taken on for their good looks, others for their strength of personality and character but temperament can often be more important than their looks.

And what about pushy mums? The mother is as important as the baby often. Because of the nature of modelling and acting work, you need to be flexible to cope with inevitable last-minute shoots and auditions. Also you need to find the whole thing fun too – to help your child stay happy and calm!

Rates of pay and hours: rates vary but some agencies pay a minimal amount for the child to attend an audition. Actual shoots pay around £50 (gross) an hour, and there is normally a two-hour minimum booking that the client will pay you for. For TV work, expect approximately £150–£200 per (five-hour) day. Don't forget that many agencies will take a commission fee from your earnings, normally at invoice stage, so you will have to factor that in too.

Child modelling is not the most remunerative of money-making schemes as most agencies estimate that even the most hard-working child will probably only earn around £2000–£4000 a year. Acting might pay more but it is also incredibly competitive. However, child modelling or acting might be a fun way to make some money especially if your little darling enjoys being a star.

Tips: both the children and their parents need to be able to cope with rejection as that is huge part of the experience. Most importantly, your baby, toddler or teenager must enjoy participating – the minute they do not, it is time to stop!

Risk	
Return	£ £ £
Time	⏱ ⏱ ⏱ ⏱
Training	📖

72
Rent your house

Drastic times call for drastic action. If you own a good-sized home in a good location then why not rent it out and downsize. Sure, the property market has bombed but it will come back. We have a shortage of housing in this country and when things are in short supply the demand increases and the price goes up. The market makes these rules. We may have to wait a few years but you will get the money back.

The good news is that because the housing market has ground to a halt the rental market for quality homes is quite buoyant and there is a strong demand.

Taking this one step further you might want to rent out your house and then take off abroad for a few years. Let all this recession business blow over and come back when the coast is clear.

Tips: talk to your local lettings agent and find out how much money you would get. If it doesn't cover the mortgage forget it. Use a letting agent to rent your house out as they will vet the applicants. Get rental insurance

Risk	🧨🧨🧨
Return	£££
Time	n/a
Training	zero

73
Rent your house as a film location

Let's face it, you're probably not going to be able to rent your home if you live in a bog standard semi in Shepherds Bush. But similarly you don't have to live in a stately home to earn money from using your house as a film location.

Film and television companies will consider all types of properties depending on the projects in hand. A small-budget documentary will pay in the region of £800 per day, while a big-name TV commercial will go up to £2000.

You will need to register your property with a locations company and they will hold your details and photographs online in their library. It's up to you to take good digital photographs and to describe why your house is a good film location; don't forget to mention quirky focal points and unusual features because this will make your house stand out from the crowd. Don't forget to include pictures of your back garden, too.

Approach as many location companies as you want, to see if they will hold photos of your home in their library: take a look at www.locations-uk.com, www.locationpartnership.com and www.locationworks.com for information (and to see the kind of competition you're up against). You want them to promote your house as much as they can to be in with a chance, so ensure they know how close you are to the centres of production like Glasgow, Bristol, Manchester and London.

In essence, you want your home to get noticed and the more unusual or dramatic your house the better. If your home is shortlisted by a production company, you will undergo what's known in the business as a 'recce' whereby production staff will visit to assess whether your home is suitable. Once successful, the location company will help to negotiate the best fee, taking their 10% commission. Be warned that a film crew is made up of a large number of people, so expect a lighting truck, a mobile generator, Charlie Dimmock and caterers to turn up, too.

Tips: tidy up before you take those all important photos and be honest in your description of your house

Risk
Return ££££
Time ***
Training zero

74
Rent your pet

Ad agencies and TV and film companies have a demand for pets with a bit of star quality. If your pets are very well trained, cute and have the ability to perform then you could earn up to £90 an hour.

It must be stressed that your pet needs to be very well trained and quite possibly a bit adorable. I have a scruffy cairn terrier that ignores everything I say and has no interests apart from sleeping, releasing evil wind and a compulsive obsession with hunting mice (I often hear her crunching their little carcases in the garden). Although I love her I know she has no star quality and will never earn me a penny from being on the telly.

You might be able to turn a few coin if your pet is unusual. Like a sloth. But don't go and buy a sloth in the hope you might be able to get it onto Taggart because you probably won't and then you end up with a very large, slow, twelve stone bradypus cluttering up your sitting room.

As usual with renting live things out be careful about getting caught up with agents and con artists charging hefty advanced fees to represent your pet. If they want money up front run a mile.

Useful info: www.theactingwebsite.com – try the animal section

Tips: only consider this if you have a truly unique pet

Risk	💣
Return	£
Time	🕐
Training	📖

75
Repair bikes

This is one that I discovered by accident. My father-in-law had a racer a few years ago and decided to store it at the bottom of the garden – not the best place to store a bike I'm sure you'll agree. By the time I got my hands on it, the tyres and seat had almost rotted away. However, being made in Nottingham back in the day when Brits actually made stuff rather than working in call centres or bundling up dodgy mortgages and selling them to my granddad's pension fund (I'm not going to forget it, am I?) the basic frame of the bike was quite sound.

So I purchased a new seat from Tesco (I thought this strange too but then Tesco sells vibrating sex toys these days so a bike seat doesn't seem too odd really) for £9 and then bought some handlebar tape and a couple of tyres off eBay for £20 for the pair. I then spent a few nights polishing it up and oiling the chain and gears and lo and behold it worked like a dream. I rode it into work a couple of times but then it rained for a few weeks solid as it tends to do in summer and my love affair with cycling came to a prompt conclusion (a bit like the guitar playing episode). So I put it on eBay and flogged it to a banker for £70. Not a bad result.

Then I discovered the tip shop. Tip shops are a new phenomenon. In the good old days you would take something to the landfill site and no matter how valuable or useful it would end up in a hole in the ground. Then everyone got green and started to recycle which made people appreciate items of value.

Now nearly every household dump has a staff of angry-looking blokes who scowl at you if you decide to chuck away your toaster. They take the toaster and put it in their little shop and then raise money for charity. One thing that the angry men are very good at saving is bikes which your fellow countrymen seem to throw away in their droves. At my local tip in London I noticed this and purchased a rather sad-looking mountain bike for £5 and took it home triumphantly. The next week I went to the tip with the sole intention of buying another mountain bike for £5. I used one to repair the other and created a newly restored mountain bike for £30. Anyone getting the hang of this. Combine the tip shop bikes, your handy work and your eBay account to create money from nothing.

Useful info: check out how much bikes go for on eBay

Tips: you'll need a good spanner set and some 3in1

Risk	
Return	££
Time	⏲ ⏲ ⏲
Training	📖 📖

76
Review music

You're passionate about music but you sound like a drowned cat when you attempt karaoke and you can't play a musical instrument for toffee. If that sounds like you then it is still possible to make money from the music industry.

A website, www.slicethepie.com, is for up and coming unsigned bands and in the scout rooms on the site you can review new music and get paid for it.

Currently scouts earn between 5p and 12p per review (simply leave a few lines reviewing the track). Your rate is dependent on the amount of tracks you listen to, and on the quality of your track reviews. It's not a massive money earner but certainly a good hobby if you like music. To date almost two million reviews have been completed on www.slicethepie.com and over £100,000 earned through reviewing on the site.

Another option on www.slicethepie.com is to invest in an artist. You can invest as little as one pound and receive free tracks, exclusive access to the artist and a share in the financial returns from album sales. For every one pound invested you are entitled to a return of 10 pence for every 1000 albums/10,000 singles sold — obviously this isn't the most fantastic return but if you are a big music fan you could take great enjoyment from supporting upcoming acts and even making some money on the way.

Risk	
Return	£
Time	⏲
Training	zero

77
Sandwiches to offices

Your average office worker will spend about £3 to £5 for lunch while at work. This normally comprises of a sarney, a pack of crisps and a can of pop. And a Crunchie on a Friday. However, with this horrible financial climate many workers are considering bringing in their own lunches to save a bit of money. But the reality of bringing in your own sandwiches is that it can get very boring. You only ever have cheese in the fridge and there are only so many cheese sandwiches a man can eat. And although you can buy big multisaver packets of crisps at the supermarket we always find that the kids eat them all on the first day. It's the same with cans of pop and chocolate. So you start out with good intentions and then before the end of the first week you're back down to Grinleys Sandwiches getting your roasted parma ham baguette again.

And then there's the social element that comes with buying lunch. The leaving of your desk, flirting with Janet in Accounts (if you are boy) or gossiping about Debbie in Sales and the awful dress she is wearing today (if you are a girl). Opening your tragic, squished cheese spread sandwiches at your desk in between spreadsheets is miserable. Mark my words, you're going to see the rise of the sandwich lady again (or in these enlightened times the sandwich person). And this could be you.

Becuase you don't have the overheads of an actual shop you can undercut the costs of their sandwiches and bring financial relief to troubled workers in your area. Start off small and pick an office complex or street to get you started (ask permission from security guards and receptionists).

Get yourself a nice big basket that can carry a selection of sandwiches, crisps and drinks. For god's sake don't do plain cheese. Be creative. Go for brie and apple or turkey and marmalade (I made that one up). Bear in mind you will need a large working area in your kitchen, adequate refrigeration and storage space, plus a way to keep the sandwiches cool before you delivering them. You can buy supplies in bulk at your local wholesalers.

There is a wealth of food hygiene regulations to bear in mind, from keeping your working area spotlessly clean to being aware of cross-contamination and food poisoning – for details and advice visit the Food Standards Agency's website at www.food.gov.uk or the Nationwide Caterers Association at www.ncass.org.uk.

Encourage customer loyalty by leaving your menus and prices when you visit. You might also like to start a 'create your own sandwich email hotline' where people can email their orders to you before a certain time if they want something specific. Check your local sandwich shops to see what they charge and ruthlessley undercut them. Buying in bulk brings down the unit cost so you can make healthy margins.

Useful info: look at www.sandwich-recipe. co.uk for recipe ideas and wholesale firm Macro can supply you with the ingredients, crisps, chocolate bars, napkins and stuff

Tips: most people seem to have an allergy these days so label sandwiches carefully. Also, presentation is key, so ensure your sandwiches arrive looking mouthwatering, rather than squashed and crumpled (try investing in some of those see-through sandwich holders)

Risk	🌑🌑☀
Return	££
Time	ⓟ ⓟ ⓟ
Training	📖

78
Secret shopper

A secret shopper or mystery shopper has to be a shopaholic's dream come true. It certainly sounds like my wife's dream job. A secret shopper is someone who is paid to shop, from trying out a new restaurant, testing the customer service standards in a supermarket, staying in a hotel or even having a pizza delivered at home.

As well as getting free food and drink in these establishments you also get paid for your time. Sounds amazing, doesn't it.

Well, yes, like all these too good to be true things it isn't quite as great as it first appears. The money isn't huge (trying to work out an average 'fee' per mystery shop is hard, but at the lower end expect to earn between £5 and £20, up to £100 a day) and be prepared to be flexible early on in what assignments you are given to ensure you get the pick of the bunch later.

Unfortunately, you also can't just sit there and lap it all up – you will be asked to report on such features as decor and tidiness, the quality of the service and the ease of finding specific products or details. The companies want all this information, and your receipts, as soon as possible, usually within 24 hours, so you'll need to set aside time to fill in the forms.

However, the flexibility is very attractive as there is no contract that says you have to do a certain amount of jobs so it is something you can fit around full- or part-time work.

Our research has shown that it also might be possible to earn some money if you are unable to get out and about. There are such things as telephone secret shoppers who conduct evaluations over the phone; postal monitoring which involves the use of a secret shopper's home address for receiving brochures and other promotional material through the post; there is also such a thing as an email mystery shopper which would require you to monitor information sent to your email address.

To get started, you have to register with mystery shopping sites such as www.retaileyes. co.uk, www.ukims.co.uk, www.cybershoppers. nopworld.com or try www.moneymagpie.com.

Secret shopping will never make you rich but if you love shopping and feel strongly about improving customer service then this can be a fun and rewarding way to make a bit of extra cash.

Useful info: there is a list of companies and information about the tax implications on www. moneysavingexpert.com

Tips: wear comfortable shoes. Take refreshments and lunch with you – you don't want to waste all the money you are earning by actually buying stuff

Risk	
Return	£
Time	⏱ ⏱
Training	zero

79
Sell your hair

Kojak, please move onto the next one. Wigs, extensions and hair-pieces are very popular and the top quality ones are made out of real hair. The selling of hair has been done for centuries and it's obvious when you consider the most important aspect of a wig is that it looks real. You can't get much more real than real hair. I mean if you use bear hair then your head is going to look like a bear's. People therefore pay a premium for real hair. To make money your hair must be at least six-inches long. Hair should also be free of chemical treatment (colouring or perming) clean and in good condition. Good quality hair can earn you up to £5 per ounce.

Useful info: www.gumtree.co.uk often has wig makers seeking hair for sale. If you are getting your hair cut don't let your hairdresser make all the money!

Tips: find a buyer *before* you cut off your hair

Risk	💣
Return	£
Time	🕐
Training	zero

80
Sell your story

The first thing that springs to mind when you hear 'selling your story' is surely kiss and tells. Every Sunday, the *News of the World* has another front-page exclusive about a footballer or politician caught with their pants down.

Some of the women involved in this tawdry trade can earn hundreds of thousands of pounds and have gone on to build, admittedly downmarket, careers off the back of their endeavours, Rebecca Loos, anyone? However, most slide back into obscurity after their moment in the spotlight. How many people will remember the name Sarah Symonds long after Gordon Ramsey continues to open new restaurants, front new TV programmes or win more Michelin stars.

There are drawbacks to this industry though – I'm sure it won't make your mum and dad proud and you may have to do the business with guys that you usually wouldn't touch with a bargepole (the name David Mellor springs to mind). Also you will probably need a modicum of beauty and a fine physique to attract their attention. So you'll be glad to know there is another way to sell your story and make some cash on the side.

Type in 'sell your story' into Google and a multitude of websites will spring up offering to sell your real-life story to national newspapers and magazine. With a daily or weekly publication there is an inexhaustible demand for real-life stories, either heart warming,

inspiring or just plain miserable. So if you feel that you have an interesting story – and this can range from love and betrayal, triumph over tragedy, traumatic experiences to the downright weird and wonderful – then this might prove a lucrative sideline.

These websites seem to be mainly run by journalists who are paid by the publications so you get the money your story is worth. Obviously you have to cope with any intrusion into your privacy and the possibility that you might upset family and friends.

Although the average payment from national newspapers and women's magazine is anything from £50 up to £500, they will pay much more for really strong stories. A particularly good true story can command anything from £500 to £1000. But payments can go into the thousands if yours is a story that everyone wants. And of course a front-page exclusive in a national newspaper may command much higher fees.

Tips: for a kiss and tell, get blonde hair extensions, a fake tan and start hanging out in nightclubs

Risk	💣💣
Return	£££££
Time	🕐🕐🕐
Training	zero

81
Selling wood

If you're prepared to put in a lot of hard work, then chopping down trees and selling the wood can bring in cash. There is a big demand for logs for open fires, wood-burning stoves and outdoor heaters like chimineas, and bags of logs sell at

£

around £5 for a 10 kg bag (15 logs or so).

Wood needs to be 'seasoned' to burn well, which means drying it out, and you should do this by cutting it into log lengths of about 12–18 inches and six inches in diameter. The cutting and splitting of logs should be done as soon as possible after the tree is cut down. For tips and advice, check out www.expertvillage.com, which also features a video on how to cut down a tree.

The best burning logs come from trees like ash, apple, pear, birch, oak and willow. Ash is also a popular wood for making kindling which sells for around £3.50 a bag.

You will need to cut down trees wherever you can, so if your's or your friends' gardens don't have trees to chop down, advertise locally as a tree feller.The downside is that you will need a licence, so visit www.forestry.gov.uk for tree felling guidelines. You'll need to get public liability insurance and hire equipment, like a chainsaw and invest in good axes, hand saws, ropes, etc and a van to remove the tree. You will also need a dry area in which to work to cut down the wood to sell. Before you chop anything down, however, check with your local council that the tree isn't protected by a Tree Protection Order or is in a conservation area.

Bag up your logs and approach garden centres, farms, petrol stations and local shops for business, aiming to sell the logs for around £3 per bag.

Tips: check carefully before you take your axe to a tree – it might be protected!

Risk	
Return	£
Time	✳✳✳
Training	zero

82

Set up a get rich quick scheme

OK, listen carefully. This scheme rests entirely on finding gullible people who are a bit lazy and a touch greedy. There are lots of them out there and modern communications have made it pretty cheap to get them on board. Lets call them members.

First, you need to get the confidence of your members. The best way is to tell them that all other money schemes are rubbish but yours is really good. Seriously, people fall for it ALL THE TIME.

Make it known early on that you are not going to ask them for money even though shortly after, er, you're going to be asking them for money. Then you need some endorsements from people who have taken part in your scheme about how good it is. Don't worry about actually finding these people because they won't exist. These other people can simply be you using different names like George and Paul and, er, Ringo.

Second, you keep talking to your members all time. Steamroller them with how exciting the scheme is. Get them to invest so much time in thinking about the scheme that when you have to levy an administration charge (remember you're not asking them for money, it's an administration charge) for £49.75 they'll be so excited about getting their ten grand that a measly fifty quid is hardly worth worrying about.

Once you've got your money you can then reveal the full details of the scheme to your lucky member; tell them to go and do exactly what you have just done to another 200 people. There's your ten grand. Most get rich quick schemes work like this: a Pyramid. You sell to the people below you who in turn sell to other people. Five per cent of people will make the money, 95% will lose money. The 5% are highly motivated aggressive sales people. You are probably not so you will probably be in the 95%. And furthermore it's illegal!

There is only one way to get rich quick and that is to be very lucky. If you are alive and in good health and somebody loves you then you are lucky. Remember that. If you want to make a lot of money then finding a get rich quick scheme will not work. Honest graft is the way to make money. If luck finds you then I'm happy for you. Alternatively you could sell sex toys.

Tips: don't fall for it

Risk	
Return	nil
Time	☺ ☺ ☺
Training	zero

83

Sell sex toys

As I have mentioned before, you can buy vibrating sex toys in supermarkets these days so it's hardly a taboo subject. According to a recent survey 35% of women own one of these gagdets so it clearly has become very acceptable. There are two ways you can make a bit of money out of this and have a lot of fun. You will find yourself very popular and in times of financial uncertainty everyone knows that sex sells!

Firstly, there is the party plan option where you get the full support of an organised brand behind you. They will provide you with training, advice, catalogues and samples and you will earn a commission on what you sell. If you have a wide social circle this is a great way to make extra money and have great fun setting up parties at people's houses. Ann Summers is the best known in this field so visit www.annsummers.com or try www.passionparty.co.uk.

The second way is to set up your own online adult toy shop. As with online dating you don't want to be paying a web developer to build you a commercial website from scratch, nor do you want to go and source thousands of products from across the world. Once again the answer is White Labelling, the practice whereby you simply badge up the front of the site and the operations behind the scenes, such as web hosting, ordering software, cash collection and dispatch (known as the back end) are run by another company. The market leader is a UK company called net www. net1on1.com. You will need a designer to create the home page for you and a templated design which will run through the whole site. Once up and running you can promote your site through local press magazines. You can also experiment with online marketing and if you already run a

website promote it to your existing members.

Tips: visit Ann Summers to see the sort of products you are going to be dealing with. Not one for the prudes out there!

Risk	
Return	££
Time	✳ ✳
Training	📖 📖

84
Small holding

For a taste of the good life, set up your own smallholding for hens or ducks. You'll need a big open space and a big enough shelter for the hens, which should be one square foot per bird with

perches and a window as the more light your hens have, the more eggs they will lay, the more you have to sell. The hens will need a nesting box and a droppings board under the perch so it is easier to keep them clean: go to www. poultryclub.org and www.country-enterprise. co.uk for advice .

Free-range hens' eggs sell for between £1–£2 for half a dozen – check out current prices with the British Free Range Egg Producers Association at www.theranger.co.uk, while the best egg-layers are the heavy breeds such as Light Sussex, Rhode Island Red and Plymouth Rock.

Ducks are much easier to look after than hens, they are less nervy and are more resistant to disease, but they don't produce as many eggs. They don't use a nesting box, just laying eggs wherever they want which means the eggs can break easily and end up lying around in poo. They have very porous shells, so their flavour is easily tainted in this way. The best egg layers are the Khaki Campbell which can lay up to 300 eggs a year. Duck eggs are a speciality and local markets and farm shops are your first port of call for sales – bear in mind that duck eggs sell for around £2.30 for half a dozen in the supermarkets.

It selling your eggs takes off, get in touch with your local division of the Ministry of Agriculture, Fisheries and Food as you will need to undergo regular checks. As you collect your eggs, name and date them and store them in a tray of sand in a cool place, ideally around 15°C. The downside is that your hens and ducks require a lot of time and care to keep them healthy and happy and they can be quite noisy.

Tips: don't get too attached and treat them as pets – they supposed to be making you money

Risk

Return   £

Time   ☺ ☺ ☺ ☺

Training   📖

85
Sperm/egg donor

The serious moral and ethical issues which surround donating sperm and eggs means that it's illegal in this country to be paid for it, despite a shortage of donors. If you want to give the gift of life you can however have your expenses paid, like travel costs and childcare. You can also claim compensation for loss of earnings, the maximum being £250. The National Gamete Donation Trust has all the information you need along with a list of licenced UK clinics at www. ngdt.co.uk.

For egg donation, harvesting requires local anaesthetic or sedation as a needle is guided by ultrasound through the stomach up into the ovaries or they are retrieved vaginally. Be aware that there are a number of risks involved from side-effects of the hormone drugs to painful sensations and bleeding.

If women are determined to make big money out of selling their eggs (they have thousands of them) then they need to travel abroad, to the US for example. Take a look at websites like www. soyouwanna.com, where it lists fertility clinics all over the US who will pay anything in the region of $2500–8000 for a donation. The downside is women will be subject to rigorous personal and medical checks, may have to spend a couple of months from initial consultation to actual donation, thus incurring living costs abroad and they will need good private medical insurance.

Some companies will help women to advertise their eggs online, like www.renewfertility. com. They will be asked to supply a donor

£

profile and will be listed with other women from all different countries and backgrounds, so if women want the cash, they'lll need to sell themselves.

Tips: don't let it faze you that you're creating life and you could combine egg donation with a great holiday abroad

Risk	💣💣
Return	**££**
Time	🕐🕐
Training	**zero**

86
Stand-up comic

If you think you've got what it takes and you're seriously funny, then have a go at being a stand-up comedian. You'll need to start off at open mic nights at comedy clubs and pubs, to gain experience, get your name known and to practise your jokes, but don't expect to earn cash yet (although you might get petrol money). Look out in the local press for venues that run this or look online at Mike's gig list on www.facebook.com or for the London area, www.spoonfed.co.uk. You'll be entertaining the crowd with other comedians, with each of you on stage for a couple of minutes.

The downside is the heckling or that nobody listens to you, so drag along a few friends to roar with laughter on your behalf.

You could attend a stand-up comedy workshop, visit London's City Lit college, www.citylit.ac.uk, for example, and read up on the course it offers. The more gigs you do and the more experienced (and funny) you become, the bigger and better slots you will get. Approach comedy clubs and comedy bookings companies for auditions, like www.

mirthcontrol.org.uk or www.laughinghorse.co.uk.

Earnings increase as your sets get bigger, so if you're supporting a well-known comedian, you could expect to get around £30, after which you would earn £100 for a 20-minute set and then on to around £300–£400 for a 30-minute set. The great thing is that this kind of work is mainly at night, so could feasibly fit around any other job you might have – and more to the point working in the day and interacting with others in your day job will surely give you ideas for jokes and stories. Take heart as Eddie Izzard, Harry Hill and Jo Brand had to start somewhere, too.

Tips: don't get into arguments with hecklers and go to as many comedy nights as you can afford to see how the professionals do it

Risk	💣
Return	**£**
Time	🕐🕐
Training	📖

87
Strip-o-gram

If you're comfortable with your body, love huge party crowds and don't mind working at night, this could be for you. There are literally hundreds of strip-o-gram companies around who you could approach to get on their books and the more you register with, the more bookings you will earn. Standard strip-o-gram requests are for a policeman/woman, a naughty nurse, a dominatrix or Tarzan, although you could specialise in a niche area in which you feel comfortable. Some agencies are on the lookout for rolypoly-o-grams and midget-o-grams, so make the most of what you've got.

You can expect to earn around £100–£120 per night, with the agency taking 20% commission. Some agencies will want to audition you first, and that could be in their office or a local strip club, so be prepared.

For ideas and inspiration, visit www.kissograms.me.uk or www.promises-agency.co.uk. Build up a portfolio of pictures of you in action to impress agencies and to try and increase your fee. Be imaginative when it comes to your act and take along any props necessary.

When you get bookings, take someone along to cut short the act if it gets rowdy or your intended recipient gets carried away. Check out the venue beforehand to ensure there are adequate changing facilities (you don't want to get into your outfit in the car park) and that the venue has given its permission for you to perform. Double check that you have the correct details for the recipient and that they are over 18. Keep it tasteful (it may be a family event) and remember you're stripping for fun and if you're cheeky enough, give out some business cards to boost bookings.

Tips: practise stripping and then getting dressed as quickly as possible

Risk	💣💣
Return	££
Time	⏱⏱
Training	📖

88
Surrogate mother

Do you think you could have a baby for someone else? If the answer's yes, then you would be giving hope to people who thought it was impossible they would ever have a family.

There are two types of surrogacy – traditional and host. The traditional way is where surrogate mothers use their own egg and the intended father's sperm, while a host surrogacy is where the egg and sperm of the intended parents are used and implanted in the surrogate mother's womb. The first is emotionally harder as the surrogate mother will be the biological parent and will have to give up their own baby, whereas the second means that the surrogate mother acts like an incubator.

You won't make any money from doing this in the UK because it's illegal to get paid for being a surrogate mother and to advertise for one. It's a different story altogether in other countries round the world like the USA and South Africa, where acting as a surrogate mother can earn you in the region of $20,000. This fee is known as surrogacy compensation and on top of this you will receive allowances for maternity clothes, housekeeping, travel expenses and so on. If you have to have a caesarian you'll be paid more because of the longer recovery time and you'll also be compensated for any invasive procedures like amniocentesis (for testing for Down's Syndrome).

The legal and moral difficulties arise whereby the intended parents may want to selectively terminate if it turns out to be a multiple birth or there is strong evidence of a birth defect. Some US fertility clinics who operate a surrogacy programme require that mothers have US citizenship, so scour the net for clinics who accept international surrogate mothers.

Useful info: take a look at www.surrogateweb.com and www.nurture.co.za for information

Tips: be prepared for the fact that you will be scrutinised intently by medical professionals, lawyers and hopeful parents

Risk 🎇🎇🎇
Return £££££
Time 🕐🕐🕐🕐🕐
Training zero

89
Take in ironing

If you're prepared to work hard (and fast) and you love ironing, then this is for you. A domestic board and iron and a few wire hangers will get you nowhere fast, as potential customers will expect a professional finish, so you will need to invest in a press, new hangers, trouser and shoulder guards as well as poly roll and an industry-standard board and iron, so go to www.ironingsupplies.co.uk for ideas. It features a starter kit for just over £50.

So how much should you charge and how much money will you make? Well, depending on the competition in your area, you can happily charge around 70p per shirt, 90p per dress and 60p per item of any other adult clothing, and charge from £1.50 to £3 for sheets and duvet covers, depending on size. Many ironing companies charge by weight, so for example, a 5kg bag of ironing will cost £5.

You need to target your customers carefully and bearing in mind that busy professionals have little time for ironing, you could offer something like a Worker's Package, and charge for 20 items to include seven shirts/blouses, five pairs of trousers or skirts, plus bedding, for around £15. Free delivery and collection will win you valuable orders, so ideally you will need someone to deliver and collect while you're hard at it. Many customers will expect a fast turnaround, so aim for 24 hours.

Take a look at other ironing websites like www.allironedout.co.uk for pricing ideas, as well as a directory website like www.ironingservicedirectory.co.uk which features its own Ironing Board Forum for lots of tips and advice on setting up an ironing service. Advertise locally and on free ad websites like yell.com and distribute flyers to affluent areas and flats.

Tips: after hours of ironing, your work area will be damp with steam, so work in a well-ventilated area

Risk 🎇
Return ££
Time 🕐🕐🕐
Training 📖

90
Talent agent

For those of you with no discernable talent there is still money to be made from the entertainment industry. In fact many of the richest people in show biz have no entertainment skills whatsoever. If you are a people person and trustworthy then this is an exciting money-making opportunity that could be right up your star street.

Contrary to popular belief talent agents are not only located in LA and New York and they don't only represent top A-list celebrities either. There are small agents located in towns and cities all over the UK and there is still a place for another one.

A local talent can be anything from a band to a comedian or a magician. Most talents are great at the entertaining bit but often need help organising the important bit like securing jobs (or bookings) or auditions or getting the cash in when the act is over.

Many large agents have started out small and start from home with nothing more than a phone and a computer. This is the beauty of this business. The start-up costs are very small and if you have confidence and the ability to sell then you could get this up and running in no time. And as with many of the jobs featured in this guide they can be done in between other commitments.

The key to be a successful agent is your professionalism and ethics. If you have these then word of mouth will expand your business. To start off with you need some key clients. Go to gigs and local venues and ask the acts if they are represented. If not make them an offer. You should get between 15% and 30% of your act's takings. You can then work with that act to promote them and get them paid

jobs. This is how you make your money. You should ask a local solicitor to draft up standard agency contract. After you have one client you should be able to use this contract for most of your new clients.

Tips: use your socialising time to go out to clubs and bars to see the local talent. Only chose an act you like yourself. If you don't rate then why would anyone else

Risk	💣
Return	££
Time	⏲ ⏲ ⏲ ⏲
Training	📖

91
Tarot reader/ medium

If you feel you have a sixth sense or you have often felt you could make a connection with the spirit world, you could set yourself up a a tarot reader or a medium. The two roles are very different and are regarded as such in the in the industry. Tarot card readers are psychic, which means with the help of the cards, they can predict what's going to happen to you and give you guidance on your life. The tarot cards are a prop and help the reader tap into their psychic ability. You can download training leaflets for free to learn what to do, visit www.tabi.org. uk, the website of the Tarot Association of the British Isles – all you'll need is software to unzip the program.

Being a medium means you are a spiritualist and that you make connections with spirits of people who have died, you believe in life after death and that spirits are trying to communicate. Often at spirtualist churches, mediums will take to the stage and address the congregation with words from the spirit world.

For more information, visit the Spiritualist's National Union website at www.snu.org.uk, which lists spiritualist churches nationwide and features adverts for mediums. You could register with them to advertise your service, which costs £24 a year. You could charge around £25 per half-hour sitting as a tarot card reader or a medium.

Psychic fairs are held often, so check out local press or visit www.psychicdirectory.co.uk for organiser's details. Stalls costs around £50 per day, and the profits thereafter are yours. Note that fair organisers will be reluctant to give stalls to unknowns or newcomers, so network with other psychics or mediums in the area to get your name known.

Tips: go for a reading to see how it's done and join your local spiritualist church

Risk	
Return	££
Time	
Training	

92
Ticket tout

It used to be that being a ticket tout was the preserve of shady characters that operated in the grey economy wheeling and dealing outside sporting venues and concerts. Well in many respects that still is the case. You need a certain strength of character to buy a load of tickets to an event in advance and then stand outside a venue in the freezing cold trying to flog them for a price that is well over that which is printed on the ticket. I'm not necessarily advocating that you embark on a career as a tout but if you have the mental stamina then give it a go.

One of the key characteristics of a tout is sensing when something is going to be in demand. For example, last year I went to see the Rolling Stones at Twickenham. For some reason the show had not sold out and there were whole blocks empty on the night. I clearly remember the desperation on the faces of the touts outside who at that point were trying (and failing) to get back what they had paid for them. They collectively must have lost thousands. You would have thought the Stones in London would have been a safe bet for a tout, but Twickenham is a rugby stadium and not a traditional rock venue. And it was a Sunday night. And Keith Richards had just fallen out of a tree and there was some doubt about whether he would be able to make the concert (or live for that matter). The net result was that people stayed away.

At the time they bought the tickets the touts were unlikely to know all of these facts but the story illustrates the inherent problems with this money-making scheme. Touting is trading and, as we know with trading, sometimes there is a high demand and sometimes there is not. Some you win, some you lose. The trick is to win more than you lose.

As with so many of these schemes the internet has made the whole thing a little easier and you don't have to be a cockney wide boy or stand outside QPR on a chilly February Saturday to participate. Venues now sell tickets directly to the public on their websites or through official agents meaning that if you have a bit of spare

**Name: Ronald
Crapes
Age: 29
Occupation:
Internet
entrepreneur**

**Internet entrepreneur and rugby nut
Ronald Crapes lives in Fulham and never
considered himself a tout until he realised
that is exactly what he is.**

I love rugby: give me 29 muddy men in a
field on a wet November and I'm the happiest
man alive. All my friends play rugby and we
love nothing better than heading off down
to Twickenham to see an international game
followed by a few hearty beverages in the pub
afterwards.

I got into making money this way quite by
accident when I purchased two tickets a couple
of years ago to see England play Ireland at
Twickenham. I bought them well in advance but
then realised that work commitments meant I
would not be able to make it. I mentioned that
I had the tickets to one of the guys at my club
and told him the price I wanted for both tickets
combined which was £100 (they had cost me
£50 each). He thought that I meant £100 each
and duly handed over £200 in cash (he's a hedge
fund manager so used to carry a lot of money on
him in those days). I had made the easiest £100
in my life.

After that I simply logged onto one of the
ticket websites and bought four tickets for a
game six months in advance. Then I kept them
in my drawer for five months and as the game
approached I marked them up £30 each. Another
£120 profit. These days I buy about 20 to 30
tickets a year to rugby games and either sell
them to friends of friends or, if nobody wants

them, I'll sell them through eBay or on one
of the ticket trading websites such as www.
seatwave.com.

I don't get involved with buying tickets for
other sports as it's not really my thing. And
I would never consider standing outside the
stadium in the cold. I like to think I'm just being
a bit opportunistic rather than a tout but then
technically what I am doing is not really any
different from those guys who do stand outside
venues. Whatever, it nets me a couple of grand a
year and pays for my post-match beers!

972482

ADMIT
ONE

972482

83

cash to invest and nerves of steel you can make a bit of money.

A good friend of mine recently purchased four rugby tickets for an England vs. South Africa game in London with the sole intention of 'flipping' them. He purchased them for £50 each and sold them for £75 each. It was a reasonably low risk transaction as he knows lots of rugby fans and was pretty confident he could sell them. And there was always the option if he could not sell them to take a few mates to the game and have a fun Saturday afternoon.

Another good friend has a phone tariff with O2. Because O2 now own a swanky arena in the Docklands they can offer their tickets to their phone customers a few days early. She was offered tickets to ACDC and although not a rock fan made a pretty good call that ACDC might not play again given that they are all 80 years old. Should they live until April 2009 then it will, of course, be a sell out. Tickets that cost only £50 a few months ago are trading on websites for up to six times their face value.

You'll need to keep your eye on up and coming events and be able to act quickly. Popular events can sell out in minutes. But if you do your research and buy wisely you could make money.

Useful info: tickets can be sold on eBay or traded (buy and sell) on websites such as www.soldouteventtickets.com or www.seatwave.com

Tips: look at venues to see who is going to play in the next 12 months and then work out how you are going to get the tickets

Risk	
Return	££
Time	🕐 🕐
Training	zero

93
Tour guide

If you have some local knowledge and time on your hands in the day then why not consider becoming a tour guide. You will need to be able to guide tourists around a specific area or attraction and give a comprehensive and entertaining tour. You can offer group tours or do tailor-made one on one packages.

Rates range from £5 per person for a walking tour through to full organised tours on a minibus or coach costing up to £500. If you are going to be driving members of the public you will need insurance cover and the usual health and safety considerations must be taken care of. Types of tour can vary from castles and stately homes to markets to countryside. I once went on a tour in London that followed in the footsteps of Jack the Ripper! Another interesting idea could be to tour the city of London at weekends pointing out banks that have gone bust.

We suggest talking to local tour guides first to establish how much demand there is and potential openings in the market. If one is struggling there might not be a big market. You should also register with your local tourist office which can be a good source of business.

You should practice your tour spiel on friends and family before unleashing yourself on the general public. Get them to try to catch you out with their questioning because the tourists most certainly will.

Tips: speak loudly

Risk	
Return	£
Time	🕐 🕐 🕐
Training	📖 📖 📖

94
Treasure hunting

It is always appealing to turn a fascinating hobby into a money-making scheme and there's an unbelievable amount of treasure just waiting to be discovered in this country. Throughout history, the British Isles have been invaded by countless armies and the ensuing battles have resulted in many valuables being scattered on the ground only to disappear just beneath the surface. Then there are the accidental losses: a ring slips off a finger, a bracelet breaks and drops on the floor.

Strangely enough, as I was researching this topic, I came across an invaluable website called www.billwymandetector.com. Yes, that's Bill Wyman, as in ex of the Rolling Stones. Turns out he is a huge fan of metal detecting. He says: "In all, I've found hundreds of coins going back to Roman Britain, as well as blades from 3000 years ago. I've also found gold coins from the 1300s which are worth £1000 each. But I'm not interested in their monetary value, it's the history that's important to me. Detecting makes history so much more interesting – it's a great hobby."

That attitude is very praiseworthy and fine if you're a former rock god but that kind of money sounds very attractive, especially as this money-making scheme is perfect for fitting into weekends and evenings.

Bill gives many useful tips for the would-be treasure hunter on his website. The most obvious one is to buy a metal detector and he has even invented his own, although it is best to buy a second-hand one when you start off.

This country is rich in history but there are areas which are particularly plentiful in pickings:

East Anglia: It's not just Roman finds here, discoveries associated with the Vikings, the Anglo Saxons, the Tudors times, the Civil War have been commonplace.

York: A battleground for much of its history, it suffered through the Wars of the Roses and the dissolution of the monasteries, before seeing a revival under Elizabeth I. York also came under siege during the Civil War.

Nottinghamshire

Kent: Its history of illegal immigrants goes back much further than our current problem – two thousand years ago it was where the Romans arrived.

Somerset

Oxfordshire

Cumbria: Its proximity to Hadrian's Wall means that the area produces many Roman finds

The Scottish Borders

Top treasure finds have included a Bronze Age gold cup – even damaged it sold for £170,000 which the metal detectorist shared with the landowner on whose property the find was made. The British Museum recently acquired a seventh-century gold sword hilt which was found by a metal detectorist who shared the £125,000 reward with the landowner. And this brings us neatly onto the code of conduct of metal detecting.

Obviously trespassing is a no-no – always obtain permission. You should note the location of any finds and report them to your local Finds Liason Officer. Acquaint yourself with the Treasure Act of 1996 which covers what is determined as treasure. Museums have the opportunity to acquire finds and the lawful finder receives the full market value. The Act also states that landowners have the right to be informed and they will be eligible for rewards.

However, even if you don't find your gold Roman coin or Anglo-Saxon sword then it is possible to make money in other ways with your metal detector. I was listening to the radio recently and Keith Chegwin, of all people, was talking about his mate who regularly takes his metal detector to the fields where car boot sales have just taken place and makes a nice sum of money every time finding the loose change that has been dropped.

Useful info: there is even a magazine for metal detecting (www.treasurehunting.co.uk). You can find out more about Bill Wyman's treasure hunting adventures in his book *Bill Wyman's Treasure Island*

Tips: really good, comfortable shoes and clothing (suitable to environment and time of year) are a necessity. Also why not join a metal detecting club in your area affiliated to the National Council for Metal Detecting

Risk	🧨
Return	££
Time	⏰⏰⏰
Training	zero

95
T-shirt printing

For the artistic people out there who don't necessarily have the skills to design their own clothes have you ever considered your own range of T-shirts? Our lives are full of mass-produced rubbish so why not fight against this and create totally unique items of clothing. You can buy standard white T shirts for £3 from a wholesaler and acrylic paint from a craft shop. Go mad and express yourself.

Outlets for your newly designed shirts are obviously eBay to start off with. Also try selling some to your friends and if you get good feedback you can then kick it up a gear and take a stand on a market stall. Covent Garden in London has loads of really cool little stands that rent for about £50 during the week.

Don't bother with this one if you have no artistic capability. Just because it's an original doesn't make it valuable. However, established unique T-shirt brands can sell individual shirts for up to £100 (although you will need to buy a premium quality white T-shirt to be able to charge this).

Tips: less is more; don't empty half a tube of paint onto a shirt

Risk	🧨
Return	££
Time	⏰⏰
Training	zero

96
Virtual assistant

Virtual assistants help small businesses who can't afford full-time administrative support or need to delegate the odd typing or admin job. You will need a spare room (or a kid-free space away from the TV and other distractions), a phone and an internet enabled computer. You should have the skills to correct unreadable emails while talking to clients or suppliers dealing in goods and services you do not understand.

If you can do all that, typically you would charge between £10–£20 per hour for routine secretarial work done by phone or email.

I believe that in a recession, the demand for virtual assistants will grow as more companies downsize and realise that hiring staff and providing offices and equipment for them is an unnecessary expenditure in a time when only the strongest (and leanest) survive.

97
Virtual economy

Some people would be forgiven for thinking a virtual economy is what got us into this recession in the first place: bankers turning the mortgages of the US poor into abstract financial ideas and selling them around the world. All very imaginative but look where it has got us.

But what we actually mean by a virtual economy is the game Second Life that is becoming increasingly popular. Second Life is an online society within a 3D world, where users, in the forms of animated avatars, can explore, build, socialize – and even make 'real' money.

Second Life has its own currency – Linden Dollars which have a real word value and can be exchanged for US dollars which can be paid into your bank account via Pay Pal.

Some people make a nice real world extra income from Second Life and a few actually make a full-time living from it.

A lot of people are just there to have a good time, to discover the islands, go to gigs, nightclubs or galleries. But, as in the real world, money does help. And so around 3500 people have got a monthly income of $10 to $50 and more than 150 residents earn between $1000 and $2000. Avatar Anshe Chung, essentially a Second Life estate agent, even makes hundreds of thousands of US dollars every year. In fact, land sales and land development is one of the most lucrative businesses in Second Life, alongside jewellery and clothing.

People are even setting up businesses in Second Life. Cory Edo – real name Sara Van Gorden – runs a business designing avatars for

However, it is important to retain a 'work mentality' – rather than lounging around in your pajamas all day, get up early, shower and dress in appropriate clothing. I've always found that if I have to work from home then putting on a pair of shoes makes you feel a little more focused. You don't have to wear a suit and tie but it is essential that you have the correct mental attitude as it will affect how you go about your job.

Useful info: www.ebs-digital.co.uk – an agency who deals with virtual assistants

Risk	💣
Return	££
Time	🕐 🕐 🕐

people new to the game.

Some argue that the current global credit crunch will drive the growth of Second Life's virtual economy. Relatively cheap luxuries like food, drink and gambling do well during recessions and dabbling in a virtual world could fit into that list of recession-proof spending quite well – it is certainly a cheap way to spend a lot of time.

Useful info: there are numerous books being published to capitalise on this phenomenon from *How to Make Real Money in Second Life* by Robert Freedman and *The Entrepreneur's Guide to Second Life* by Daniel Terdiman

Tips: operating in Second Life can become addictive which means you could start taking the first life (the real one!) less seriously

Risk	
Return	£
Time	☺ ☺ ☺ ☺
Training	**zero**

98
Waiter (part time)

From coffee shops, to bars and restaurants, you can take your pick of part-time waiting work. It's flexible and you can choose to work as little as one night a week. Providing you have some experience, are prepared to work hard and have a sociable manner, most employers will take you on.

The drawback is that you'll only earn around £5–£6 an hour and you're on your feet for all your shift, and the shift can be a long stretch, say from 5pm till midnight. You can expect to earn tips so you'll need to have great people skills,

making them feel special and not rushed. You'll be expected in most cases to provide your own uniform – the obligatory black trousers or skirt, white shirt and black shoes. In fact, the better your appearance, the more likelihood you'll get work.

In big restaurants and hotels, you will probably be asked to provide ID like a passport, a national insurance number and references. Check out www.clickajob.co.uk, www.careers-jobs.eu and www.gumtree.com for current vacancies or your local press.

The key quality most waiters must possess is keeping cool under pressure in busy periods, so that orders are taken correctly and mistakes are avoided. You'll encounter stressed kitchen staff, so be clear and concise with any extra instructions or customer requirements. Also, you'll be required to clear tables, take payment and make toilet checks. Remember at all times that 'the customer is always right'– deal with disgruntled or drunk customers in an efficient way and score brownie points with the manager. You'll also need a good memory for the specials and an enthusiasm for the food or drinks that you're serving – and expect at least a 10% tip from each customer.

Tips: practise hovering discreetly at home and carrying platefuls of food

Risk	
Return	£ £
Time	☺ ☺ ☺
Training	📖 📖

99
Wedding make-up

Probably another one for the ladies. Can I

also point out at this stage that if you have absolutely no interest in make-up or beauty then don't advertise yourself as a wedding make-up person and have a crack at it because you could quite literally ruin the most important day of someone's life!

However, if you have a natural flair for doing make-up and styling this could be for you. You can charge up to £200 for doing make-up for weddings, parties or special occasions. Often the work is weekend or evening based so you can fit it in around other jobs or commitments.

Academic qualifications are not as important as creative and practical skills but it is recommended that you take some sort of course because many can tell you about the business aspect as well as the technical aspect. There are various courses, from the study at home type, to the short college courses for a few hundred pounds right through to a two-year course at The London College of Fashion.

This is a competitive business. Equipping yourself with the necessary make-up and brushes is expensive, as is getting photographs of your work for your portfolio (a collection of photos of your best work).

How do you get paid work? Word of mouth and showing your portfolio to prospective clients is important. Always take your portfolio round in person. This is an industry in which it is vital to get on with people and where self-promotion can get you a long way.

Risk	
Return	££
Time	⊙⊙⊙
Training	📖📖

100
Writer

You're probably thinking 'nahh, I could never do that'. Well, that's what I thought and then in September 2008 my first book came out. I have three O levels and precious other qualifications. It just turned out that I could write and it never really occurred to me to try to do it until I was 37. So have a crack. It's not made me rich but it contributes towards the household bills and I love doing it.

Since writing that book I constantly carry around a little pad in which I scribble down ideas for novels I might never write but it is a hobby that I shall continue for the rest of my life.

There are various ways you can get started. Why not contact your local magazines. Avoid nationals to start with because they get bombarded with writers. Small local magazines are probably hard up and are more likely to use local writers and pay them next to nothing. Pitch them an idea you would like to write about and if they give you a trial agree a word count and have a go. Pick a topic that is on your mind, sketch out the points you want to cover and then write it without worrying too much about the word count. Then go to bed. Then look at it again with a fresh pair of eyes the next day. Show it to friends or family and see what they think.

You're unlikely to have the stellar success that JK Rowling had (but if you do, remember I got you started) but it can be very rewarding. And books make you immortal.

Useful info: there are online courses you can take such as www.writersbureaucourse.com and your local college will have introductory courses. If you find you enjoy it there are journalism courses all over the county

Tips: keep a little pad with you to make notes. Make sure you use the spell check on your PC

Risk	
Return	££
Time	⊙⊙⊙⊙
Training	📖-📖📖📖

101
Crime

I had to put this in because once you open your mind to making a bit of extra cash the lure of criminal activity will cross your path. It may seem easy and the likelihood of getting caught slim, but don't fall prey to easy temptations. Buying a dodgy bike from a bloke in the pub, importing heroin, people smuggling, arms dealing and contract killing are all tempting but ultimately against the law of the land (although curiously 24.9% interest on a Laura Ashley Credit Card is permitted and apparently legal

– whassallthatabout?).

If you break the law some of you will get away with it, some will get a slapped wrist, others will get incarcerated and some (if really dodgy) will find yourself wearing concrete slippers at the bottom of the Thames (see any Guy Ritchie film for further information on villainy and the myriad of sticky ends that one is likely to encounter). If it's illegal avoid it.

Tips: crime doesn't pay – just ask the Krays

Risk	💣💣💣💣💣
Return	**probably nothing**
Time	**lots of prison time**
Training	**depends on the crime**

£ Notes

Useful Info

www.equity.org.uk

29 Fashion

www.fashionspace.com

www.oxfam.org.uk

30 Find a friend a job

www.zubka.com

31 Fishing and hunting

www.environment-agency.gov.uk

www.hotbarrels.com

www.shootinguk.co.uk

www.sportinggun.co.uk

www.thefield.co.uk

www.ukfoodonline.co.uk

www.fishupdates.com

32 Flower arranging

www.nafas.org.uk

www.easyfloristsupplies.co.uk

www.smithersoasis.com

33 Focus groups

www.insightfocusgroups.co.uk

www.qualityeye.com

34 Foraging

www.wildmanwildfood.com

www.goselfsufficient.co.uk

35 Fossiling

www.ukfossils.co.uk

36 Freecycle trading

www.freecycle.org

37 Fruit and veg picking

www.pickyourown.org

www.pickingjobs.com

www.anyworkanywhere.com

www.moneymagpie.com

39 Gift cards

www.fotopic.net

www.artymiss.co.uk

www.essentialcraftbits.co.uk

www.craft-fair.co.uk

40 Grant grabbing

www.energysavingtrust.org.uk

www.moneysavingexpert.com

41 Handy man/man with van

www.ultimatehandyman.co.uk

www.handymanplus.co.uk

www.vanman.co.uk

42 Home shopper

www.mysupermarket.co.uk

www.boots.com

43 Home tutoring

www.personaltutors.co.uk

www.firsttutors.co.uk

www.localtutor.co.uk

www.setyourrate.com

43 House clearance

www.thrifty.co.uk

45 House sitting

www.homesitter.co.uk

www.g-angels.co.uk

46 Internet surveys

www.lightspeedpanel.com

www.yougov.com

48 Knitting agent

www.dailyknitter.com

50 Local councillor

www.communities.gov.uk

51 Make chutney and jam

www.bakersandlarners.co.uk

www.lakeland.co.uk

www.bbcgoodfood.com

www.jam-recipes.co.uk

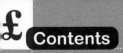

Contents

Useful Info